Revolutionary War Patriots

BLADEN, ROBESON, CUMBERLAND, SAMPSON, AND DUPLIN COUNTIES, NORTH CAROLINA

by Dr. Rev. Carolyn Cummings-Woriax

RoseDog Books

PITTSBURGH, PENNSYLVANIA 15238

RoseDog Books
585 Alpha Drive, Suite 103
Pittsburgh, PA 15238
Visit our website at *www.rosedogbookstore.com*

ISBN: 978-1-64957-805-1
eISBN: 978-1-64957-825-9

Revolutionary War Patriots

BLADEN, ROBESON, CUMBERLAND, SAMPSON, AND DUPLIN COUNTIES, NORTH CAROLINA

RESEARCHER, WRITER, AND COMPILER:

REV. DR. CAROLYN CUMMINGS-WORIAX

ASSISTANT:

SGT. (RETIRED) WILLIAM RONALD "PETE" BELL

DESCENDS OF PRIVATES: PVT. JOHN BROOKS AND PVT. SAMUEL BELL,

RESPECTIVELY

JULY 26, 2019

WASHINGTON'S PRAYER FOR THE NATION

Almighty God, we make our earnest prayer that Thou wilt keep the United States in thy holy protection, that Thou wilt incline the hearts of the citizens to cultivate a spirit of subordination and obedience to government, and entertain a brotherly affection and love for one another and for their fellow citizens of the United States at large.

And finally that Thou wilt most graciously be pleased to dispose us all to do justice, to love mercy, and to demean ourselves with that charity, humility, and pacific temper of mind which were the characteristics of the Divine Author of our blessed religion, and without an humble imitation of whose example in these things, we can never hope to be a happy nation.

Grant our supplications, we beseech Thee, through Jesus Christ our Lord. Amen. (Written at Newburg, June 8, 1783, and sent to the Governors of all the States.)[1]

[The *Song and Service Book for Ship and Field: Army and Navy*. Edited by Ivan L. Bennett, Chairman of the Editorial Committee, United States Government Printing Office, Washington, 1942. Copyright, 1941, by A. S. Barnes and Company, Incorporated.]

---

[1] Bennett, Ivan L., ed., *The Song and Service Book for Ship and Field: Army and Navy*, A. S. Barnes and Company, Inc., 1941.

IN MEMORY OF

This special collection of Revolutionary War Patriots is written in memory and the history of both writers' ancestors: Progenitor Private John Brooks, Bladen County, North Carolina and, Progenitor Private Samuel Bell, Halifax, Virginia.

Both patriots left a most remarkable and meaningful history and account of their notable service to their country, America, in her early efforts to free herself from the British rule of Kings and Queens from a Parliamentary system to a Democracy government and, the ultimate desire to become a nation of freedom for all persons regardless of color, creed, sex, or race.

It is indeed my desire to dedicate this project to both families and especially to those fore-fathers who taught us as children: "To always know who you are and whose you are."

SPECIAL THANKS

First, I want to thank my children, families, and friends for their prayers, patience, support, faithfulness, and endurance during my time spent in long hours in critical research, travel, writing and rewriting this essay.

Secondly, I wish to thank Sergeant (Retired) William Ronald Bell who provided assistance with wealth of knowledge of the Bell family, the Saddletree Community, military information, reading and rereading. In addition, his encouragement and support in writing this essay.

Lastly, I wish to thank Jane Blanks Barnhill for her valuable knowledge of the Bell family and her resource, *Sacred Grounds162 Lumbee Cemeteries in Robeson County*, 2007. Also, thanks to my son, Fredric Carroll Woriax, MD, who serves as Lt. Col. in the US Air Force Air Corps, Langley AF Base, Virginia, and, daughter-in-law, Velinda L. Woriax, PhD., Biology Department Head at UNC-Pembroke University, Pembroke, North Carolina, for their gifts and guidance in the art of English and Composition.

"When did the wondrous mystic art arise of painting speech, and speaking to the eyes? That we by tracing magic lines are taught how to embody and color thought?"

[Anonymous]

TABLE OF CONTENTS

INTRODUCTION

This essay attempts to list the orthography of the names of American Indians Soldiers, as written in the Muster Rolls of the Militia documents, of North Carolina (NC), South Carolina (SC), and additional states. Indian Soldiers who served with White and Black soldiers in the Colonial Wars, and/or the American Revolutionary War (1765-1783) of the Thirteen Colonies it is said to have ended in NC about (abt.) 1782. NC is now known as the "First in Freedom" state, earned the name, "Tar Heel" as a joke between the soldiers in the Confederate War. It is said that Jefferson Davis had purchased all the tar in the state, to which General Lee responded, "God bless the Tar Heel boys."[2]

In critical research, this writer discovered that many of the former soldiers who served in the Colonial War, Indian Wars, and the Revolutionary War remained in the boundaries of North Carolina and South Carolina, especially in Bladen County, NC and the Great Pee Dee, Marlboro County, and Richland County, SC. One elderly woman in the Affinity section of Bladen County [now Robeson County] shared that she saw Revolutionary War soldiers searching for Tories soldiers around her family's home.

Many of the local soldiers were held as Prisoners of War (POW), Killed in Action (KIA), Death by Wounds (DOW), and/or were Missing in Action

---

[2] The Robeson County Area, *The Historical News*, p.7, Hiram, GA, April 2019.

(MIA). This writer's ancestor (6x) John Brooks was held as a Prisoner of War in Florida and hospitalized at Pennsylvania (PA).

Those who remained in Bladen County received Land Grants for their service to the country. Land Grants were awarded in Bladen, Brunswick, Carteret, Columbus, Cumberland, Duplin, Onslow, Richmond, and Sampson County, NC. Their descends continue to live on the lands and homesteads which were established in the late 1770's and early 1800's.

This writer, in her critical research for this project discovered that most of the early Indian soldiers in Robeson County were among the ancestors or were progenitors of the early Indians living in the following counties in NC: Bladen, Duplin, Halifax, Robeson, Sampson, and Warren and various counties in Virginia, South Carolina, and other states throughout the United States of America.

Valuable resources include, Eric G. Grundset. Ed. and Project Manager, *African American & Native American Patriots Appendix of the North Carolina Daughters of American Revolution War Soldiers* (NSDAR), Ancestry.com, and other early historical listing of military engagements, for example, the Indian Wars and Colonial War historical documents. Especially, the importance of the following two books, Francis Hawks, *History of North Carolina*, Vol. I and Vol. II and The Right Rev. Alexander Gregg, D.D., *History of the Old Cheraws*.

These two books contain a wealth of material which correlates to the early Robeson County Indian family culture, customs, and traditions.

Also, the majority of this essay historical information was gleaned from writer's Cummings-Brooks Family historical documents and the author's private non-published writings: *The Early American Indian Patriots and Soldiers Roster in North Carolina and South Carolina, The Samuel Bell Historical Family, The Creation of An Innovative People 1700-1887: The Shaping of a New Territory: Robeson County, NC, and Early Land Grants and Deeds*.

However, readers should be quick to note that many of the early Revolutionary War Patriots came from Halifax County, Isle of Wright, and the Roanoke River, Virginia, Surry County and Warren County, NC. Halifax

County, NC was formed from Edgecombe County, NC in 1758. At the close of the Revolutionary War, many of the soldiers remained in the local area after being issued Land Grants in Bladen, Brunswick, Cumberland, Duplin, New Hanover, Robeson, Sampson, and additional Counties. These men intermarried with the women living in the lower North Carolina and upper South Carolina. Others brought their families with them during the war, while others who came into North Carolina came through waves of migration to America.

Note: In this document names and surnames suffered corruption from their original spelling in historical documents, US Federal and county censuses, grave markers, and family documents. Writer will use said name as written in such documents.

Disclaimer: If your direct family member or an indirect known soldier connected to any soldier who served listed in this essay in the Revolutionary War is not listed in this essay, it is because writer failed to discover their name or names while searching military documents, state and local library archives, church records, family records, cemeteries, interviews, and/or personal knowledge, ancestors, relatives, or neighbors to those who served.

BOOK I

REVOLUTIONARY WAR PATRIOT
PRIVATE SAMUEL BELL S6598

PRIVATE SAMUEL BELL S6598

The following essay is derived from the documents pertaining to Private Samuel Bell, his Military records, and the genealogical accounts of his families, the Elizabeth "Betsy" Gilbert Family and The Holmes Family, in addition to researcher's resources.

Samuel Bell (Halifax, Surry County, VA, May 1749-abt. 1835, NC), S6598

The Elizabeth "Betsy" Gilbert Family: Samuel Arthur Bell (1749-1806)

The Holmes Family: Samuel Arthur Bell (1749-1834)

This essay focuses on the Revolutionary War soldier, Private (Pvt.) Samuel Bell S6598, and his descendants. Also, included in this essay are other Revolutionary War Patriots associated with Samuel Bell and his family members. These soldiers were comrades: those who served as witnesses and/or bondman's in marriages, or intermarriages, land deeds, and their continuation of friendship in Bladen, Robeson, Cumberland, Sampson, Duplin, and additional counties in North Carolina.

In addition to these patriots, additional names of Revolutionary War Patriots who played an important or a minor connection to Pvt. Samuel Bell and his descendants in Robeson, Cumberland, Duplin, and Sampson County, NC, are included in this essay.

A.W. [Angus Wilton] McLean (20 Apr 1870-21 Jun 1935), president, Bank of Lumberton, Lumberton, NC, wrote a letter dated 14 Sep 1914, to the Honorable Commissioner of Indian Affairs, Dept. of the Interior, Washington, DC, in reference to Pvt. Samuel Bell, Pvt. John Brooks, Pvt. Richard Bell, Pvt. Primas Jacobs, Pvt. John Hammond, and additional American Indian Patriots who fought in the Revolutionary War.[3]

Lastly, writer discovered that both Pvt. Samuel Bell and Lt. Hardy Holmes families were former members of the "non-white members separated out" from the Saddletree Colored Church formerly known as Hammon Church, December 5, 1873.

John Hammons, Revolutionary War soldier was issued a 200-acre land grant, 7 Jul 1750. The Hammons Church, according to early land deeds, was built on John Hammonds' property in the Saddletree Community. Its land deed is suggested to be the first church land deed in Robeson County. John's descendants continue to serve as pastors in the general area.

Pvt. Samuel Bell, entered the Revolutionary War under Colson, 7 Feb 1782, for 12 months. It is suggested that he married Elizabeth "Betsy" Gilbert (1751-1845). Writer failed to discover a marriage certificate for Samuel and Elizabeth "Betsy" Gilbert Bell. She was the mother of Isabel Robert Cummings (1783-1817) and Anna Cummings (1822). Searching NC Marriages, writer discovered an Isabel Cummings marriage to Asa Carman, 25 Nov 1803. Carman served in the 1812 War.

Searching online documents and Ancestry.com, writer discovered one Anna B. Cummings (9 Oct 1822), the daughter of Samuel Cummings and Elizabeth Cummings, Jonesboro, Maine. The Betsy Gilbert family suggests Samuel Bell died about (abt.) 1806. The Hardy Holmes family suggest Samuel died abt. 1834.

Elizabeth Bell Gilchrist married Thomas Cummings. Their children were: Francis Cummings (d. 1832), never married and Harmon Cummings

---

[3] Cummings-Woriax, *Early American Indian Patriots and Soldiers Roster*, p. 95.

(25 Mar 1756-19 Feb 1851). Writer has failed to discover the relationship of Hardy H. Bell to Mary/ Nancy Bell or to Isabel Cumins (1783-1817), Rebecca Bell (1822), Anna Cumins (1824), or to Elizabeth Bell Gilchrest (1751-1845).

Searching her roster of the Early American Indian Patriots, this writer discovered one Pvt. John Barksdale Cummins, who married Isabel Ivey, 30 Sep 1806, Abbeville, SC. Also, Pvt. John Cummings, who served in the Revolutionary War. He married a (NKA) Capps.

And, Aaron Cummings, from Sampson County who served in the 4th Company, 1812 War.

In the Early Halifax Listing 1784-1787, writer discovered the following names: George Bell, Elisha Bell, John Blunt, Sarah Bell, Elisha Bell, Elias Foort [Fort], Sugans Foort [Fort], John Fort, John Bell, William Swett, Abraham Swett, Allen Sweat, Thomas Hogg, John Kinchen, Trustram Drake, William Cummin, Thomas Locler, Willis Fort, Moses Gains [Goins], and Allen Fort.

Samuel Bell, according to his War Pension documents was born (May 1749), in Surry County, VA. In 1807, Samuel Bell made application for his Revolutionary War Pension while in Robeson County. Samuel stated that he had served with the following soldiers: Jesse Manuel, Hardy Holmes, Joseph Hester, John Hesters, Isaac Hammonds, and Moses Carter in the Revolutionary War. Reading his military documents, Samuel Bell signed his name with the letter, S, "ɛ" lying flat.

Listed under Pierces Register #91678. Bell, Samuel, Pvt., commenced 3 Apr 1831, Revolutionary War soldier, entered through the NC Continental Line, Sampson County, NC. At (85) years-of-age, Samuel Bell's pension became effective, 4 Mar 1831. His last date of payment, 3rd qtr. 1835, Fayetteville, NC. The above information for Samuel Bell was adapted from the following resources: Samuel Bell's Revolutionary War Pension Record, 1832; The NC Daughters of American Revolutionary War Soldiers, *Appendix*, North Carolina African Americans and American Indians in the Revolutionary Era, *Forgotten Patriots*, p. 570. And, writer's unpublished resource, *The Early Indian Patriots*.

Samuel Bell served in the Colonel (Col.) Lytle's NC Regiment. Writer's maternal great-uncle, Joseph "Joe" Brooks, the son of Alexander "Sandy" and

Effie Hunt Brooks, was the great-grandson of Private John Brooks. Joseph wrote a letter to the War Pension office on behalf of Samuel Bell's pension.

On 27 Feb 1933, A. D. Hiller responded to Joseph Brooks letter stating that Samuel Bell's Revolutionary War pension became effective, 6 Sep 1833.

> While residing in Sampson County, NC, Samuel Bell volunteered in the Revolutionary War, Feb 1782. His rank, Private. He served in Captain Coleman's Company under Major Griffith McCree and Colonel Lytle in the North Carolina Troops. Pvt. Samuel Bell was discharged Jan 1783. He continued to live in Sampson County after the war. In 1807, he moved to Robeson County, NC. He was living in Robeson when his pension was executed August 31, 1832. No information on his family available. For further information on Pvt. Samuel Bell, please contact the comptroller General, citing this information. His certificate was issued, 6 Sep 1833, rate 36.6 per year, commencing 4 Mar 1831, Act., 7 Jun 1832, NC Agency [Fayetteville].[4]

Writer discovered George Hammond (25 Feb 1750), Richmond, VA, who served as a Revolutionary War soldier. He was wounded in the battle at Eutaw Springs, 8 Sep 1781. His parents were: William Hammond and Winifred Milner. George married Sarah Dickson. He died (10 Apr 1840), Anson County, NC.

Writer suggest that George was a sibling to Isaac Hammond, p. 17. Isaac gave the name, George Hammond as a namesake to his son. No doubt, Isaac was a member of the Hammonds family living in Anson County, NC.

Samuel Bell was listed in the Sampson County Early Tax List 1784. Writer discovered a marriage between Samuel Bell and Polly Jones, 15 Jan 1814, Cumberland County, NC. Polly Jones' son was Edward Bell.

Samuel Bell lived in Sampson County, NC according to the 1790 Sampson County census. He was Head of (10) Free People or Persons of Color

---

[4] Cummings-Woriax, *Early American Indian Patriots and Soldiers*, p. 78.

Household Members. In the 1800 Sampson County census, Samuel Bell was Head of (15) Household Members.

Another, Samuel Bell received a Land Grant, Halifax County, 1786.

The Robeson County Court Minutes 1797-1843 list Hardy Bell as a "Boy of Color" bound to Samuel Bell, 27 Aug 1810, p. 217. The practice of being bound out was a common practice among Indian, White, and Black families and their children in Robeson, Cumberland Counties, and in early colonization in early America. For example, in 1786, John Oxendine, age (4) years-of-age was bound to Neil McCrainy and in 1788, Nancy "Nance" Oxendine who was only (18) months-of-age, the daughter of Betsy Oxendine, was bound to James Dyer. Both, John and Nancy were bound in Cumberland County, NC.

No doubt, John, Nancy, and Betsy Oxendine were family members of Charles Oxendine who was living in early Cumberland County. James Dyer, no doubt, served in the Revolutionary War. He was issued several Land Grants in Cumberland, 1790 and 1801. Writer discovered Dyer listed in the early 1767 Cumberland Tax List.

In 1795, the *North Carolina Central and Fayetteville Gazette Newspaper* published an ad in which a Nancy Oxendine was labeled a Free Negro and a Mustie servant woman.[5]

In writer's unpublished book, *Creation of An Innovative People*, Nancy Oxendine died at age (97) years-of-age. She was listed as a Slave. Charles Oxendine married Abby Cumbo, the daughter of John Cumbo, who served in the Revolutionary War, Halifax, NC. John's parents were Gideon (1702) and Ally Cumbo.

Also, a Richard Dryer married Elizabeth Cumbo (1688), VA. Perhaps, Richard was an ancestor to James Dyer.

In the Robeson County Court Minutes, the following two orphans, Elkanah "Elkaney" Hammonds (1797-1845) and Jacob Hammonds were bound to Captain (Capt.) Jacob Blount, 1 Sep 1819. Capt. Jacob Blount, a Tuscarora

---

[5] North Carolina Central and Fayetteville Gazette Newspaper, 1795. Https://www.ancestry.com accessed: 20 Jul 2017.

Indian, served in the NC Militia, 1777. He was formerly from the Pitt Precinct. He later moved near Pvt. Samuel Bell at the Great Coharie, Duplin County, Clinton, NC. Perhaps, this Jacob Blount was a family member of Chief Tom Blount, Tuscarora Indian, who lived near Fort Christanna, Virginia (VA).

Writer discovered an Eleanor Blount (1781) living in Duplin County, NC, 1850. Writer failed to discover her connection, if any, to Jacob Blount. Also, Philip Blount, Jr., whose parents were: Philip and Margaret Blount, in the Saddletree Community. Philip married Catherine McNeill, whose father was: Archibald McNeill.

Writer failed to discover the relationship of Elkanah and Jacob Hammonds to Jacob Hammonds listed below. Elkanah married Orra Roberts, 20 Jan 1820. Their daughter, Sally Sarah Hammonds (1827-1926) married Quincey Godwin. Elkanah Hammonds was enumerated 7 Aug 1820.

Jacob Hammonds was listed in the 1790 Robeson County census as Head of (4) "Persons of Color." His daughter, Phereby "Ferebie" Hammonds (1824-1882) married Alfred Chavis, a Civil War soldier. On 26 Nov 1789, Jacob Hammons was issued a Land Grant for 100 acres on the westside of Saddletree Swamp and an additional Land Grant for 50 acres, 18 Sep 1795, at Ten Mile Swamp and Poplar Pole Branch.

Hammonds, Jacob, Pvt., served in the 4th Regiment (Jones') Georgia Militia in the 1812 War.

Hammonds, Ephraim, Pvt., served in the Revolutionary War. He was listed as a barber. He and his brother, Isaac Hammons [Manuel] were Mulattoes having no African blood in them as stated by Daniel Graham, register of the Treasury.

In 1820, Ephraim Hammonds was Head of (12) Household Members; and in 1840, he was Head of (10) Household Members in Kentucky (KY).

Samuel Bell married Nancy Carter, Cumberland County, 17 Sep 1819, bondsman, Ephraim Hammond. Ephraim served as a Trumpeter in the Revolutionary War. Ephraim Hammonds married Rebecca Bell, 26 Feb 1812, bondsman, Thomas Sampson. Rebecca (1746/1750) is assumed to be a sister or daughter to Samuel Bell by the Gilbert family.

Nancy Carter and John Carter were listed as Gingaskin Indians from VA.

In the Cummings-Brooks Family resource, Thomas Sampson married Elvie Hammonds (1778-1827). Their son, Henry H. [Hammonds] Sampson (23 Dec 1804-3 Apr 1874) married Nancy Carter (1802). Their daughter, Angeline Sampson (1837) married William B. Oxendine.

Writer discovered William B. Oxendine listed as a merchant in the Branson Directory.[6]

Thomas Sampson was enumerated 7 Aug 1820. In 1830, he was Head of (2) Household Members. Thomas married Rachael Chavers, 6 Jun 1827, Robeson County, NC according to the Graham-Chavers Family history.[7]

On 20 Oct 1787, a Nancy Carter was listed as the daughter of John [David] and Lydia Brayboy according to David Brayboy's Last Will and Testament, Robeson County. David and Lydia's sons, Stephen Brayboy (1819) married Mollie Edwards. The couple lived in Laurel, Indiana (IN). David Brayboy (1840), a barber, lived in Jefferson, IN. David and Lydia's additional children were: Patta, Patience, Milly, and Levi.

David was issued a land grant for 100 acres near the five-mile swamp beginning at the Pugh Corner, 10 Apr 1763. John [David] Brayboy was issued a 100-acre land grant on Bugg Swamp, 2 Apr 1767.

In the 1820 census, p. 17, Samuel Bell was Head of (2) Household Members – 1 male over 45 and 1 female over 45 – Free people of Color. Samuel Bell was enumerated 7 August 1820, Robeson County, NC.

Samuel Bell lived near to Colonel (Col. William) Hugh Brown [1750, per military record; d. 1794]. Hugh was Head of (9) Household Members and (13) Slaves. Hugh Brown, Jr., married Catherine Black, 28 Oct 1832. Witness was J. F. Barnes. Col. Hugh Brown was issued multiple Land Grants in Bladen and Robeson Counties.

Col. William [Hugh] Brown raised a large family and owned many slaves. He served in the Revolutionary War through SC. In 1810, Hugh Brown was

---

6 Branson's North Carolina Business Directory, Robeson County, p. 561. Http://interactive.ancestry.com/10160dvm
7 Cummings-Woriax, *Creation*, pp. 58 & 445.

the owner of 1050 acres of taxable property in Captain Watson's District. In the 1820 US Federal census, younger Hugh Brown lived in an area between Philadelphus and Buie. A neighbor was Samuel Bell. Hugh died, 18 May 1851. The Hugh Brown Cemetery setting is located on the Brown's property in a grove of trees in the Philadelphus Community. The tombs and grave markers are grand and majestic.

Hugh Brown's grandson, Neill Archie and Margaret Carmichael Brown's daughter Ethel Brown, lived in one of the family's older homes in the Prospect Community. She never married. She was a social voice for the Indian people in their plight, including writer's father. After WWII, writer's parents left Newark, Delaware, to live in a share croppers' house on Ms. Ethel's farm in the Prospect Community.

Ms. Ethel continued to provide support to this writer long after her first son was born in 1960. In years past, writer's two paternal uncles, Newton Cummings and Baker Ray Cummings, bought land acreages from the Browns in the Prospect Community.

Today, writer's neighbors are the descendants of both the Browns and the Peter Dial families who have intermarried or were born into or out of wedlock. These two families have been farmers and neighbors since their early settling in Prospect and, Bear Swamp-St. Anna Communities.

In 1830, while living at Neils Creek, Cumberland County, Samuel Bell was Head of (6) Household Members – 1 male 50-59 and 1 female 40-49.

On 16 Nov 1790, Samuel Bell was issued 100 acres of land near the Great Chorea [Coharie], Sampson/Duplin County, Clinton, NC. And, on 7 Jun 1832, Samuel Bell received Land Grants, Act. 7 Jun 1832, Land Grant Sampson County, NC.

On 1 Aug 1832, Samuel Bell moved to Sampson County, NC.

Felix Bell received a Land Grant for 100 acres, 17 Dec 1803. Relationship to Samuel Bell unknown.

A younger Felix Bell's (3 Aug 1835-7 Feb 1914) parents were: William and Rebecca Bell, Sampson County, NC. Felix served in Company B, NC 51st

Infantry Regiment, Confederate War. He enlisted 28 Apr 1862, Wilmington, NC; discharged 15 Jan 1864.

Hesekiah Bell (1750) was living in Sampson County in 1784. On Nov 15 1803, Martha Bell was listed as administrator of Hesekiah's estate. He was possibly a relative to Samuel Bell.

Samuel Bell relatives or children: Arthur Bell (1751-1775), served in the Revolutionary War. Also, Benjamin Bell served in the Revolutionary War. The Holmes family resource lists a Samuel Arthur Bell living in Burke County, GA.

Benjamin Bell's parents were: Richard and Candis Bell.

William Bell (1798) married Rebecca (1798). His father was: Thomas A. Bell (8 May 1856-3 Jan 1926), whose parents were: Nathan Bell and Julia Boone. William served as a Confederate soldier. He married Mary Ann Moore (1847-15 Jan 1899).

In critical research, writer discovered the following Bells: Penelope (1784); Martha (1813); Walter (1829); and, Martha E. (1834) living in Duplin County, NC, 1850. Also, George Bell (1790); Betsy (1794); Tery P; George; and, Tehetha.

Blount, Jacob, Captain (Capt.), [Tuscarora Indian], served as a Porter to his officer and as the Paymaster for the NC Militia, 1777. Jacob formerly lived in the Pitt Precinct. He later lived near Samuel Bell, Coharie, Duplin County, Clinton, NC. Jacob Blount, Sr., served as a witness in a Robeson County court case on 4 Mar 1831. The court voucher read that Jacob lived 3.5 miles from the courthouse and for his service he was paid travel for (7) seven miles. Jacob Blount's daughter, Celia Blount (1770-1830) married John Willis (1775-1844).

Benjamin Blount appeared in the Robeson County Court on 5 Nov 1803. In Francis Hawks book, *History of North Carolina*, "List of Freeholders in 1723," Vol. 2, pp. 62-67, writer discovered one Benjamin Blount (Beaufort) and Jacob Blount (Pitt), and many other persons who were later living in Bladen and Robeson Counties, NC.

According to *Branson's Business Directory*, Benjamin Blount lived in St. Pauls, NC. Could he be a relative to Mary Blount? She appeared in the Robeson County court as a witness that Charles Townsend shot into the home of

Mary Cumbo on 10 Apr 1831. Robeson County Court document states that Mary Cumbo and Mary Blount lived in the same house 12-14 miles from Lumberton, NC. Mary Cumbo was the widow of Gideon Cumbo. Their daughter was Elizabeth Cumbo.

In the 1850 census, Mary Cumboe, age 75, pauper, lived in the home of Alfred Townsend, dwelling #100, family #100, Southern Division, Robeson County, NC.[8]

The Robeson County Court Minutes read that the following two orphans, Elkanah "Elkaney" Hammonds (1797-1845) and Jacob Hammonds were bound to Jacob Blount, 1 Sep 1819. Elkanah married Orra Roberts, 20 Jan 1820. He was enumerated 7 Aug 1820.

Jacob Hammonds was listed in the 1790 Robeson County census as Head of (4) Persons of Color. On 26 Nov 1789, Jacob Hammons was issued a Land Grant for 100 acres on the westside of Saddletree Swamp and an additional Land Grant for 50 acres, 18 Sep 1795, at Ten Mile Swamp and Poplar Pole Branch. Jacob Hammonds was the son of John Hammons, the Revolutionary War soldier living in the Saddletree Community.

---

[8] Cummings-Woriax, *Creation of An Innovative People*, p. 252.

Pvt. John Hammons, S8654

On May 1852, John Hammons applied for his military pension, stating that he had fought in the Revolutionary War abt. 6 years under Col. Dobson, Major Jones and others. He served in the following battles: Cow Pens, Beatties Bridge, Guilford Court House, and Gates's Defeat. His pension amounted to 2728 pounds 9 shillings –3281 pounds 11 shillings, 5 pence. [ADDRESS FOR PRIVATE USE]

Hammon, John (abt. Jan 1738/1748- Jan 1760-Oct 1858), Pvt., served in the Revolutionary War through VA, 2nd Regiment, Co. B, Calvary, in the NC line. He lived in Robeson County and also Anson County, NC. When applying for his war pension, a witness, Levi Locklear, testified that John was blind. According to his military history, John Hammons died (120+) years-of-age, while living in SC.

John Hammons served under Col. Dobson, Major Jones and others. Sworn statements by: James D. Bridgers, John McCallum, Levi Locklear, Robert Bullard, Elias Bullard, Clias Paul, and J. C. Acford [Alford]. This writer home sits near to the Elias Bullard's homestead, farm, and the Elias Bullard Family Cemetery.

John Hammons is recognized as the Progenitor of the Hammonds in the Saddletree Community.

Writer discovered Revolutionary War soldier, John Hammon listed in the Robeson County Will Book #1, p. 125, who in his Last Will and Testament left his son, Samuel Hammon as executor. John's wife was Christian [Locklear]. Their children were: Elijah, Henry, two grandsons William, and Cornelius Jackson, the sons of Thomas Avenith Jackson, Jacob, John, Norfleet, Seradford [Stanford], and Helen. Apparently, his two sons, Elias and Enoch Hammon were deceased.

Did Thomas or John Jr., marry Avenith Jackson, 1 Mar 1811? Avenith's sons were: William and Cornelius Jackson. John Jr., and Avenith's son was Henry Hammons.

The following names were Revolutionary War Patriots who fought alongside with Pvt. Samuel Bell in the Revolutionary War. These soldiers were mentioned in Bell's deposition for his war pension: Pvt. Jesse Manuel, Lt. Hardy Holmes, Pvt. Joseph Hester, Pvt. John Hesters, Pvt. Isaac Hammonds, Capt. Jacob Blount, and Col. Hugh Brown and others who are mentioned throughout this essay.

Writer discovered Hardy Bell, Lt. Hardy Holmes, John L. Holmes, and Capt. Jacob Blount, living in Robeson County, in 1830. In 1790, Hardy Holmes was the Head of (3) Household Members and (14) Slaves.

Hardy Holmes was a witness to Captain (Capt.) John E. Willis (NC, abt. 1759-22 Apr 1802, MS), Revolutionary War soldier and Asenath Barnes (NC, abt. 1863-1807, MS), marriage, 1779. Asenath signed her Last Will and Testament, 1 Dec 1806, Natchez, MS. [ADDRESS FOR PRIVATE USE]

Also, listed was Pvt. Jacob Lockerman [Locklear], Duplin County, who served on the "Little Coharie," Sampson County, as a Loyalist in the Colonial War. Lockerman was listed as French.

Jacob Lockerman, no doubt, is the following, Lockerman [Locklear], Jacob (1754), whose parents were: John Locklar (1720-1790) and Elizabeth Knight Oxendine (1725-1790), Edgecombe County, NC. Jacob fought in both the Tuscarora War and the 1812 War.

One Archibald Bell, former Revolutionary War soldier, Household Member of (1), self was issued a 200-acre land grant described as a desert, 29

Dec 1755. It reads that an Indian stated that the land was Arable [fit for crops]. His pension commenced 5 Mar 1833, at (76) years-of-age.

Writer discovered a younger Archibald Bell who served in the Civil War through IN. He entered 1 Jul 1863 at the age, 63. Archibald's (NC, 18 Jan 1820-5 Nov 1890, IN), parents were: William Bell and Aladelphia Speakes.

In the 1880 Indiana census, dwelling #143, lived Archibald Bell (NC, 1820, age 60) listed as Head of (6) Household Members. His wife, Elisabeth (VA, age 52) and their children: Rosa (age 18), J. John (age 17), Elmore (age 15), and Ida (age 13), lived in Lafayette, IN.

In dwelling #137, family #146, lived E. William Bell (IN, age 27), Susan (IN, age 23), and R. Ora (age 1). William list his father as being born in NC and his mother as being born in VA. Evidence is clear that E. William Bell's parents were: Archibald and Elizabeth Bell.

An additional family in dwelling #136, family #141, F. John Redding (NC, age 44), daughters were: A. Phebe (age 22), M. Susan (age 14), and M. Ida (age 10), all born in IN.[9]

Jesse Manuel (1746/1750-25 Dec 1834; Alt. date 27 Mar 1835), Pvt., S41808, served in the Revolutionary War, Bladen County, North Carolina-line and in the 1812 War. His parents were: Ephraim Emanuel (1730-1804) and Emelia (1752). Jesse married Elizabeth Lovice Holder (1778-1850).

In 1810, Jesse lived in Cumberland County and Sampson County. He was Head of (6) Household Members. On 6 Oct 1820, at (74) years-of-age, Jesse Manuel was living in Wake County, NC. There he applied for his war pension. In his disposition, he stated that he had lived in Raleigh city limits for three years and then moved about seven miles out of Raleigh and had lived there for the last seven years.

Jesse Manuel married Eliza Harris, 15 Aug 1825. His third wife was Elizabeth Webb, 3 May 1844. In 1830, Jesse Manuel was living in Robeson County as Head of (6) Household Members. According to Robeson County

---

[9] 1880 Lafayette, Indiana Census

court archives on March 1830, Jesse Manuel brought assault charges against Jesse Jones.

John Hester (1754-18 Feb 1819) received a Land Grant, Bladen County, 29 Dec 1778. He married Comfort Jane Johnson, whose parents were: Thomas Hester and Sara Hodges. John's son was David Hester.

John Hester (1754-18 Feb 1819), Sampson County, married Rebecca Redding (1749-1834). Their children were: Hannah (NC, 1788-29 May 1868, FL), Ephraim, Thomas, John, Comfort, Sarah, Miriam, and Mary. Could Rebecca Redding be related to John Redding who left NC and settled in IN? He lived next to the Archibald and Elizabeth Bell family in IN.

Hester, Joseph (1750-1802), Pvt., served in the Revolutionary War. According to documentation, Joseph Hester married Elizabeth Parker, 4 Jul 1781, Granville, NC. Eliza was born in Pasquotank, NC, 6 Nov 1759. Elizabeth made her second widow application for Joseph Hester's pension in 1845. Joseph Hester died in 1802, Granville, NC. Joseph Hester's Probate Will date 1802, signed by Elizabeth Hester and Elijah Parker, Nov 1802.

In 1790, Joseph Hester was Head of (4) Household Members. And in 1810, a younger Joseph Hester was listed as Head of (6) Household members.

Joseph Hester married Elizabeth Lois Epps, Granville, NC, 10 Oct 1817. Elizabeth Epps (1716-1760), Nansemond County, VA, was the daughter of Daniel Eppes [Epps], a Revolutionary War soldier. He served in the Pamunky [Pamunkey] Artillery, VA. Eppes [Epps] is an Indian surname discovered in Halifax.[10]

Daniel Eppes [Epps], (1671-1753), served in the Colonial War/Revolutionary War soldier through the Pamunky [Pamunkey] Artillery, VA. His parents were: John Eppes and Mary Kent. Daniel married Mary Jordan (1676-1755).

Joseph entered the Revolutionary War twice in 1782. Joseph Hester was issued a Land Grant for 20 acres, 15 Aug 1800; another 100 acres, 27 Nov 1804; another 100 acres in 1809; an additional 87 acres, 15 Jul 1824; another additional 100 acres, 30 Nov 1840 in Bladen County, NC.

---

[10] Cummings-Woriax, *American Indian Patriots*, p. 27.

Joseph Hester's second application for his Military Pension was made by Elizabeth Hester, who was a widow in 1845.

Hester, Benjamin, Pvt. In 1781, he entered the Revolutionary War through Sampson County, NC. Benjamin served in the 10th Continental Line Regiment for 12 months. Benjamin married Molly Dyer, 2 Dec 1778, Granville, NC. In 1810, he was Head of (19) Household Members.

It is possible that Hester's wife, Molly Dyer, was the daughter or a relative to James Dyer living in Fayetteville, Cumberland County, NC.

Writer was informed that a section in the city of Lumberton was formerly known as Hester Town. Hester Town's present location is where the Robeson County Public Library now sits.

Hammonds, Isaac (1750-1 Aug 1822/1833), Pvt., W7654, served in the Revolutionary War as a Fifer. Isaac married Dicey McLean (1776-10 Oct 1852), Cumberland County, NC, 1787 or 1 Jan 1794, Cumberland County, NC. They were the parents of three (3) children: Asberry Hunt Hammonds (1833-1918), Rachel Hammonds, and George Hammonds.

In 1790, Isaac lived in Cumberland County as Head of (5) Household Members. Dicey applied for Isaac's pension Sep 1849. She stated that Isaac Hammonds died in 1822 and she later married Anthony Hammonds, 1827. He died in the same year.

In 1840, Dicey McLean Hammonds [a widow] lived in Cumberland County as Head of (3) Household Members. Her daughter, Rachel or Elizabeth Hammonds (1808), and two grandchildren, John H. Hays (1837) and Henrietta Lomack (1839), the daughter of Rachel and Enock Lomack.

Enock Lomack was the son of William Lomack, S41783, Revolutionary War soldier. Dicy Hammonds' Last Will and Testament, 8 Oct 1852, contained specific instructions for her daughter, Rachel and her husband, Enock Lomack, and Rachel's heirs, to receive the remainder of Isaac Hammonds' Military Pension, balance of $1201.

Enock and Rachel Lomack's son, David Lomack married Mary Simons, 17 Jun 1813. Mary's parents were: Ransom and Lucy Simons.

Freeman, Jacob (1774), Pvt., married Dicey Hammonds, 19 Dec 1825, Cumberland, NC. Jacob Freeman served as a Revolutionary War soldier. Jacob was granted a 40 acres Land Grant, 31 Dec 1792. The land was located on the west side of the great swamp. No doubt, this was the Great Cohere River, Sampson County, NC.

Nelson Freeman married Rebecca Bell, 4 Oct 1842, Cumberland County. Could she be the widow of Ephraim Hammond?

Jacob Freeman married Beedy Taylor, 18 Nov 1843, Robeson County. Jacob Freeman was enumerated 7 Aug 1820. In 1820, he was Head of (5) Household Members and (1) Slave.

Hammons, Shadrach (1750-1824-1757-1852), Pvt., served in the Revolutionary War through VA Militia, 6th Regiment. He was the son of Mary Hammons. Shadrach married Susannah Delila Carter (1780-1865). He was enumerated 7 August 1820, Edgecombe County, NC.

On 30 Oct 2017, while researching *Abstracts of Wills*, Edgecombe, NC, 1733-1856, p. 513, by Ruth Smith Williams and Margarette Glenn Griffin, at the Old Edgecombe County Historical Library, Asheville, NC, writer discovered the following documentation regarding one, Delilia Revel.

In the 1828 Aug Court, Book F, p. 92, 26 Aug 1824, Shadrack Hammons, presented his Last Will and Testament. He listed his three children: Uridice, Willis, and Elijah, to receive his estate. Also, included in his will was Delila Revel and her three daughters: Susanna, Rosanna, and Elizabeth to receive items from his estate. Delilia [Hammons] Revel was Shadrach Hammons sister. Shadrach Hammonds and Delilah Hammonds were the children of Mary Hammons and Humphrey Revell (1790-1832), 28 Dec 1811, Edgecombe County, NC.[11]

Did Mary Hammond marry a Carter?

The following article appears in Elizabeth Shown Mills book, *Evidence Explained: Citing History Sources from Artifacts to Cyberspace*, 2nd ed., Revised 2012, p. 395.

---

[11] Cummings-Woriax, *Creation*, p. 536.

1. Nash County, North Carolina, Bill in Equity, 1834-1835, case no. 6, Delilah Revel v. Nicolas Lewis & Others; Folder: Delilah Revel, Nash County Loose Papers; North Carolina State Archives, Raleigh.[12]

Humphrey was the son of Elijah Revels (1745-1897) and Dolly "Dollie," (1750-1811). He was born in Bertie or Nash County, NC (1790) and died (30 Nov 1832), Edgecombe County, NC. Humphrey and Mary lived in Edgecombe County. Humphrey Revell was a Revolutionary soldier. He married Delilah Hammons or Hammonds, 1811. She was born in Edgecombe (1790- Apr 1835) and died in Nash County, NC. Their children were: William N. (1812-1850); Elijah Revel (1817-1895), who later became a preacher; Sally (1818); and, Mary E. (1819). Both boys were minors at Humphrey's death in 1832. Delilah's second marriage was to Nicholas Lewis, 1832, Edgecombe County.[13]

Samuel Bell was living in Robeson County according to his, 4 Mar 1831, Pension deposition. He stated that he was given leave to go home after the battle at Charles Town, but never received word to return to war. Samuel received the following Land Grants: Grant No. 407, Rockingham County, 100 acres, 4 July 1800, both sides of Jacobs Creek, entered 10 April 1784.

Also, Grant No. 297, Sampson County, 100 acres, 16 November 1790, on the westside of the Great Cohere [River], entered 16 October 1788.

In critical research this writer discovered that Samuel Bell had married multiple times. He married Nancy Carter, 17 Sep 1819, the daughter of Jane Carter (1787), Sampson County. In an earlier marriage, Samuel married Polly Jones, 11 Jan 1814. Polly previously married John Thomas, 13 Nov 1813.

In the 1880 census, Cumberland County, one Polly Jones [Polly Ann Oxendine], (1863-1 Mar 1940) was listed as a widow. Her parents were: Anderson Hammonds (1840) and Nancy Hunt. Anderson was the son of Ollen and Silvia Roberts Hammonds. Polly was living in the home of her nephew's family: John Roberts, Mary West Roberts, and their children, Cattie, John, Fany, and Ida Roberts.

---

[12] Mills, Elizabeth Shawn Mills. *Evidence Explained: Citing History Sources from Artifacts to Cyberspace*, 2nd ed., Revised 2012, p. 395.
[13] Cummings-Woriax, *Creation*, pp. 536-537.

Silvia Roberts was the widow of Pvt. Ishmeale [Ishmeal] Roberts (1750-1826), a Revolutionary War soldier. Their son was Zachariah Roberts. Zachariah gave his son the name, Ishmeal Roberts, II.

Ishmeal Roberts made his Last Will and Testament 12 Jul 1826. Apparently, he was an heir of Pvt. Kinchen Roberts, Halifax, VA, Revolutionary War soldier, Third Regiment. In 1800, Kinchen was issued a land Grant in NC. Kinchen was living in New Bern at his death abt. Oct 1784.

Orra Roberts (1805) was formerly Orra [Arra] Hammons, who married John William "Luke" Carter. Their daughter, Carolina [Caroline] Carter Hammons (1839-26 Dec 1930), died at 104 years-of-age. Luke and Orra's daughter, Sarah Margaret Carter, married E. J. [Edward James] Emanuel. Luke Carter (1796) married Elizabeth Woodell, 29 Apr 1852.

Elizabeth Woodell married Cyrus Locklear. Their daughter, Holland (29 Mar 1886-21 Jun 1918) married JC "Jerry" Bell. Holland Bell was buried in the Saddletree Church Cemetery.

James Madison Emanuel's (1825-1895) parents were: Shadrack Manuel and Nancy "Dicy" Hardin.[14]

Manuel, Shadrack "Shadrach" (1781-1880), enlisted in the Revolutionary War through Sampson County, NC. His parents were: Nicholas Manuel and Mahalie Bungey. Shadrack married Sarah Gay (McGee). His second wife was: Susan Manior [Maynor], 27 Dec 1859.

The above marriages were performed in Cumberland County, NC. Both the Gilbert Family and the Holmes Family suggest that Samuel Bell married Elizabeth "Betsy" Gilbert. That she was the mother of Hardy Holmes Bell. Writer failed to discover Hardy Bell's mother name.

Stephen Thomas (1832-1953) and Cintilla [Till, Matilda, or Sentecca] Manuel/Emanuel (1834-1896) were the parents of James Robert "Jim" Thomas (1854-1931). He married Arrie Bell Chavis (1863-1953). Arrie Bell's parents were: Alfred Chavis (1825-1864) and Phereby "Fesbee" Hammonds (1824-1882), 30 Dec 1843. Pherby's parents were: Elkanah Hammonds (1797-1850) and Orra [Arra] Roberts (1805).

---

[14] Cummings-Woriax, *Creation*, p. 486.

It has been suggested that Phereby Hammonds was buried in the Amos Bell Cemetery, Saddletree Community but that cemetery through the years has been demolished and turned into a hog pasture. Ms. Barnhill informed writer that Phereby's grave marker was not found among the few remaining grave markers in the Amos Bell Cemetery.

Arie Bell Chavis' father, Pvt. Alfred Chavis (1822-1864; alt. date 6 May 1862), entered the Civil War through Bladen County, NC. He served in Company D, South Carolina 26th Infantry Regiment. He also served in the Third Artillery, 40th State Troops, NC. Alfred's parents were: Daniel Chavis and Caroline Carter.

Alfred was killed in action (KIA) near Petersburg at the Clays Farm, VA, 1864. Alfred married Phereby "Ferebie" Hammonds, 30 Dec 1843, NC. Their daughters: Arrie Bell Chavis married James Robert Thomas, and Flordia "Fleridy" married Wilbur Warriax/Woriax.[15]

Phereby and Alfred's son, Cain Chavis (1856) married Isabella Carter, 12 Dec 1882, Robeson County, NC.[16] Isabella's sister, Fannie Carter married Walter Wilkins. She was buried near the St. John's River in GA. A brother, Floyd Carter, the eldest son, was killed and buried in FL. Another sister, Sarah Eliza Carter married Malcom Carter, 14 Feb 1885, moved to and lived in Covington County, AL.

It has been suggested that Cain Chavis entered Robeson County from Oklahoma (OK). Writer in critical research discovered Cain listed in various states with different spelling. In 1860, Kain and 1870, Rain, Robeson County; 1900, Kang, AL; 1910, King Chavers, and 1920, Kain, FL.

Reviewing her unpublished book, *Creation of An Innovative People*, this writer discovered that an extended Chavis family, Patrick Chavers (1807) and Elizabeth West, who formerly lived on the Bull Swamp, SC, moved to OK. The family filed the Dawes Claim for their Indian recognition. They lived and died in the OK Indian territory.

---

[15] Ibid, pp. 35 & 521.
[16] NC Marriage Records, 1741-2011, Https://www.ancestry.com, accessed: 24 Jul 2019.

Also, George Washington Lowrie, and additional Indian men [Revels, Chavis, Dial, and/or Locklear] traveled with him to OK in the mid to latter 1800's. Their mission was to check on the status of the Indians [Old Settlers] who had earlier moved westward and to bring back news to their family members who remained in Robeson County.

Cain and his family lived in Pensacola, FL. At his death, Cain was buried in the Jay Cemetery, Pensacola, FL. Isabella (19 Feb 1860), St. Pauls, NC, lived and died in FL. She was buried in the Cora Baptist Church Cemetery, Pensacola, FL.

Cain and Isabella's son, Thomas D. Chavis (28 Aug 1886-28 Sep 1952), served in the US Army, WWI. Thomas D. married Bertha Mae Nowling. His second wife was Liz Booth. He was buried in the Jay Cemetery, Pensacola, FL. He was enumerated in 1900, Creshaw County, AL.

Additional members of the Chavis family were the following persons.

Amasiah "A. R." or "Amos R." Chavis, Jr., (1897) married Pearlie Mae Woriax (1898), 4 Oct 1919. Amos R. (18 Jul 1861-11 Jul 1953) married Elizabeth Oxendine. Pearlie Mae's parents were: Rev. Edward Frank "EF" Woriax and Matilda Jones, the grandparents of writer's deceased husband, Frank Woriax, MD.

The Thomas and the Woriax families migrated to and lived in Greene and Cocke Counties, TN. James Robert Thomas and the younger Woriax children moved to NC with their widowed mother, Betsy Woriax Babbs. Betsy married Butler Babbs, a merchant in TN. Betsy's children, E.F., Wilbur, Amanda Belle, Hannah, Susan, and Joseph Elmer returned to Robeson and Sampson Counties in the late 1880's, without Babbs. Writer has failed to discover information on the two additional children, William Woriax and Mary Woriax, who were left in or they were bound out, adopted, or had died at an earlier date in TN.

James and Arrie Bell's daughter, Florida "Fleridy" Thomas (1880-1966) married Wilbur Warriax, a brother to Rev. E. F. Woriax. James and Arrie Bell's son was James Braxton Thomas (1886-1924).

Pheraby Hammonds Hardin (1800-1900) married Michael Emanuel (1787-1860). They were the maternal grandparents of James Henry Bledsole (1886-1924), Sampson County, NC.

James Henry Bledsole married Hannah Woriax/Warriax, the sister to Amanda Belle "Amandy," Wilbur, Joseph "Joe," and Rev. E.F. Woriax/Warriax. James Henry and Hannah lived in, died, and were buried in Sampson County.

Carter, Moses, Pvt., S41470, served in the Revolutionary War, through the 1st Regiment NC Continental Line, 1 Aug 1782 for 18 months. He married Ann Walker, 17 Jun 1779, New Hanover. In 1780, he was living in Anson County. In 1800, Moses was Head of (8) Household Members. Moses signed his name with an "M." He was issued a Land Grant 1805.

In 1790, Moses Carter was Head of (9) Household members. Moses married Tobiha White, Craven, NC. Moses married Matilda Hammon from Beaufort, NC, the daughter of Virginia Hammond (1805).

On, 24 Oct 1820, Moses Carter, at (83) years-of-age, applied for his War Pension. His war pension commenced 1821. The war pension payment, 1st qtr. 1822, Fayetteville, NC. Lawyer, Hardy L. [Lucian] Holmes, Sampson County, served as property distributer of Moses Carter property, 26 Oct 1820. Moses Carter died 18 Mar 1818. Hardy L. was the son of Hardy Holmes, Revolutionary War soldier [17]

Carter, Henry, served in the Revolutionary War. Henry Carter lived in Sampson County in 1800 as Head of (8) Household Members. He married Sarah Carter, Nov 1821. Henry Carter (d. 25 Dec 1848). Sarah Carter made application for his pension in 1848. Apparently, Henry and Sarah were the parents of (6) children.

Hammonds, Absalom [William], (NC, 1775/1783), Pvt., served in the Revolutionary War through Burke County. In 1781, he lived in Cumberland County. Absalom married Mary Williams from SC. Mary was buried at Hunt's Mill, Chesterfield County, SC. Absalom applied for his military pension 25 Mar 1833, Sullivan County, TN, age 76. Absalom lived near the VA & TN line.

Their daughter was Jeannie Lynn Hammonds who married a John Brooks. Absalom's War Pension application was rejected. It is suggested that he also married Sila Clark.

---

[17] Cummings-Woriax, *American Indian Patriots*, p. 17-18.

Writer has reached the conclusion that Shadrack, Delila, Isaac, Ephriam, and Jeannie Lynn were the children of [William] Abaslom Hammons/ Hammonds and Mary Williams from SC.[18]

---

[18] Cummings-Woriax, *Creation*, p. 536.

The Hardy Holmes "Hardie" Bell Family

Hardy Bell (1 Jan 1786-28 Apr 1866) was born in Sampson County. He died in Robeson County. Hardy's parents were: Samuel Arthur Bell (1749-1834) and Elizabeth "Betsy" Gilbert. Hardy Bell's spouses: Patsy Pool, Sarah "Sallie" Parker, and others, according to North Carolina censuses.

The Robeson County Court Minutes Archive 1797-1843 lists Hardy Bell as a "Boy of Color" bound to Samuel Bell, 27 Aug 1810, p. 217. Tradition suggest his mother was Jane Bell, a daughter or relative to Samuel Bell. Normally, this applies to children bound out to others as servants or to work on farms. [ADDRESS FOR PRIVATE USE]

Correction and Evidence: Apparently, the suggestion that Jane Bell was the mother of Hardy Bell, is similar to those who believe Hardy's mother was Elizabeth "Betsy" Gilbert. This writer researched various county censuses for a Jane Bell to which she discovered, most Jane Bells' were listed in England or migrated to America from England.

Hardy Bell (abt. 1770-28 Apr 1866) married Pasty Pool, 1818, Johnston County, NC.

Reading the 1820 census, Hardy Bell was Head of (5) Household members. It is interesting to note this Hardy Bell was listed as a Free Colored Person – Male 14 thru 25; his spouse – 26 thru 44; 2 males under 14; and 1 female under 14. Therefore, this Hardy Bell's birth was abt. 1795; the spouse 1794; and the 3 children abt. 1806.

After much deduction, this writer has reached the conclusion that the 1 Free Female 26 thru 44 was an older female. No doubt she was the mother of the 4 children, Hardy Bell, 14 thru 25, 2 boys, and 1 girl, all under the age 14.

Did the above Hardy Bell marry Sarah "Sally" Parker, 1820, and/or Sally Porter,1800, Cumberland County, NC? If Hardy Bell did marry Sally Porter, 1800, then he would be Hardy Bell born abt. 1770.

Writer has reached the conclusion that the early Parkers listed in this essay could be the children of Joseph and Elizabeth Parker.

In 1830 and 1840 censuses, Hardy Bell was Head of (10) Household Members. He lived next to Lt. Hardy Holmes, Pvt. John Holmes (1777), and Capt. Jacob Blount. Additional Blount's were Philip Blount (1740-1801) and Margaret whose children were: Philip Blount, Jr., John (1772-1816), and Celia Blount (1770-1830). Celia married John Willis. Their son was Daniel Willis.

Sherman Jacob Blount (1834) no doubt, was the son of Jacob Blount who lived in Sampson County. He served as a Private in the Confederate War in the Company H, 61st Regiment and in the 20th Regiment. Sherman was killed in action (KIA), 1865.

Blount, [Sherman] Jacob, Pvt., served in the Confederate War 1865. J. C. Blount (1836) lived with the Stephen and Ann Jones family in Sampson County, NC.

Holmes, John (1756), Bladen County. In the summer of 1777, he entered into the NC Continental Line through the Capt. Mills Co., 18 Dec 1781 for 12 months. He served for four years as Justice of Peace, Brunswick County. His 2nd pension application date was 7 Feb 1852. According to his record, John Holmes did not receive any county land of the US, dated 30 Apr 1829.

Duplin County Pvt. John Holmes is often confused with Pvt. John Holmes (abt. 1758), Brunswick County, NC. He did not receive any county land of the US, dated 30 Apr 1829. [See Pvt. John R. Holmes, 5173, Revolutionary War deposition on p. 28.]

While living in Duplin County, John Holmes married Swanee [Florence Swan] McLean (May 1881-24 Jul 1914), the daughter of Henrietta Brigman.

John Holmes and Swanee's daughters were: Emma Laura, Ethel, and Dovie Holmes (1898). Dovie married Tommie Allen (1 Mar 1895-5 Oct 1963). His parents were: Sandy Allen and Josephine Holmes. Josephine was the daughter of Macon Holmes and Margaret Young.

Also, Theopholus Barfield (1785), served in the 1812 War. He was living in Duplin County in 1850. Could he have been a relative to either Cade Barfield or Needham Barfield? Both Barfields served in the 1812 War.

Pvt. Gabriel Holmes (21 Dec 1786-23 Sep 1848), served in the Continental Line through Sampson County. He married Mildred L. Molson [Mabson], (1791-22 Aug 1835), Sampson County, then Wilmington, NC. Their daughters were: Mary N. Holmes and Margaret Holmes. And, their son, Gabriel Holmes, Jr., (1769-26 Sep 1829) married Mary Hunter, the daughter of Theophilius Hunter, Revolutionary War soldier, Sampson County.

The following, Holmes, Gabriel, First Sgt., served in the Revolutionary War. He married Lucy Drew, 6 Nov 1824, Halifax, NC. The surname Drew is an Indian surname, Halifax, NC.

Writer failed to discovered the relationship between the two Gabriel Holmes or if they were the same person. One younger Gabriel Holmes served in the 46th Regiment Infantry in the Civil War.

However, she did discover that Gabriel, Jr., and Mary's son, Theophilus Hunter Holmes (13 Nov 1804-21 Jun 1880), was given his maternal grandfather's name. Gabriel, Jr., who served as the 21st Governor of NC, term 1821-1824. Gabriel, Jr., married Mary Smith, Wake County, NC. Gov. Holmes, Jr., was buried in the John Sampson Cemetery, Clinton, NC.

One John Sampson, a Pamunkey Indian, served as a commander in the Spanish War. His wife received his pension payment in King Williams County, VA.

Major Theophilus Hunter Holmes, served in the Indian War and the Mexican War. He was buried in the MacPherson Presbyterian Church Cemetery, Fayetteville, NC.

Writer asked the question as to why Pvt. John Holmes failed to receive any county land or pension from the soldiers Old Money Account of the NC

Line. Searching Fold3- Military Records, 30 Sep 2019, writer discovered abt. fifty pages regarding John Holmes application for his war pension and as to why it was rejected. The following account is a synopsis of the fifty pages.

Pvt. John Holmes R. 5173

Pvt. John Holmes at the age (80) eighty years-of-age made application for his Revolutionary War Pension, 21 Dec 1839. John's daughter, Mary Jane Beasley, reapplied 8 Aug 1851. Through deduction, John Holmes was born abt. 1758 at Black River, Bladen County. He entered service in 1777. At his deposition, John stated that he entered under Captain Robert Ellis at Ft. Johnson, Brunswick County, NC and that his years of service of 22 months were at Ft. Johnson. Additional officers were: Lt. Mantz, James Smith, and John Devane. John shared the following account: A British ship approached the fort and blew-up the Maga line. Some 80 to 90 men were in the magazine, but all escaped except for Lt. Devane, Sgt. Denny, and three others. These men were taken aboard the ship as Prisoners of War (POW). They were taken out to sea and kept for days. Later, the soldiers were put ashore on a tiny point nearer to Wilmington. John states that he was given his discharge paper by Capt. Ellis, but he lost the paper and that he did not serve in any other battles, only at Brunswick.[19]

Searching for his name among the Revolutionary War pension records, his name did not appear on any roll of agencies in any state. John Holmes stated that Natanaiel [Nathaniel] Potter and John Anderson could testify that he fought as a

---

[19] Fold3- Military Records, Ancestry.com, 30 Sep 2019.

soldier in the Revolutionary War. Also, Benjamin Lock, Towns Creek [Brunswick County]. Lastly, John shared that his name was listed on a pauper's list.

Writer did discover while reading war pensions that on 1 Apr 1852, $80.00 was approved. However, the war dept. agent did write that he had located another Pvt. John Holmes listed under Capt. Mill Co., who enlisted 18 Dec 1781 for 12 months. Writer failed to discover the correct date of John Holmes death. For all purposes, his death was prior to 1852.

Writer, in her research, located another John Holmes born (abt. 1805). In the 1790 Brunswick County census, one John Holmes was Head of (1) Household Member. In addition to the following persons listed in the 1790 census, Joseph Holmes, Samuel Bell, Sr., Samuel Bell, Jr., Nathaniel Bell, and James Bell, Sr. These Samuel Bells can be found in this writer's essay, *The Historical Samuel Bell Family* (private resource, non-published).

In critical research, this writer discovered in the Records of Deeds, Book "S," p. 156, at the Robeson County Courthouse, 27 Sep 2018, Samuel Bell's transfer of his property to his son, Hardy Bell, 13 May 1819. The first part, Samuel Bell and the second part, Hardy Bell. In the consideration of two hundred dollars ($200.00) to be paid in hand by Hardy Bell. Hardy Bell and his heirs as administrators of a parcel of land located south of Ten Mile (10-mile) Swamp which lies at the property corners of David Allison and Wiley Rozier.

On 16 Nov 1790, Samuel Bell was issued 100 acres of land near the Great Chorea [Coharie] River or Indian settlement, Sampson/Duplin County, Clinton, NC. And, on 7 Jun 1832, Samuel Bell received Land Grant in Sampson County. No doubt, these Land Grants were issued for his service in the war.

Writer discovered a second land deed, "O," p. 233, 27 Feb 1806, which was a transaction between Thomas Barnes and John Blount of Robeson County, NC; one-part, Samuel Bell and the second part, the others. Thomas Barnes and John Blount sold the land to Samuel Bell for the sum of sixty-one pounds, six shillings, and six-pence. Samuel Bell and heirs listed as administrators of the land parcel which lies south of Ten Mile (10-mile) at the corners of Baxley and Newbury. The land parcel consists of two hundred and twenty-three acres (223) and was patented at Raleigh, 8th February 1798.

Thomas Barnes and John Blount release the property to Samuel Bell and his heirs free and clear from all lawful claims. Thomas Barnes and John Blount signed and sealed the transfer of property in the presence of Thos [Thomas] Shanks, January Term 1807. The deed transfer must be registered. J Mc (surname unreadable). [ADDRESS FOR PRIVATE USE]

Blount, John (d. 24 Jan 1778/15 Jul 1788), Pvt., entered the Revolutionary War under Doherty. He lived in Robeson County. His son-in-law was John Stagner. His sons were: Elias, Philip, and Jacob Blount. An ancestor, John Blount (1718-1790) was known as the "old man in war."

Blount, John, served in the War of 1812 through the 5th Company, Sampson Regiment. According to his date of birth (1718) and the 1812 War, John Blount was (94) years-of-age. Therefore, he earned the title, "old man in war."

In 1820, John Bell, lived in the Capt. Cowiart's [Cowart's] District, Cumberland County, NC. In 1840, John Bell (1784-1860) had moved to Sampson County. Writer discovered John Bell's Last Will and Testament, 12 May 1788, in Deed Book #1, p. 16, Duplin County, Bladen County, and Hanover County. His witnesses were: Samuel Atkinson, Charlotte Atkinson, and Henson Pope.

In Deed Book, p. 88, 6 Feb 1804, Mary Bell, in her Last Will and Testament, left her son, Joseph Atkinson as executor, and her additional children. Her son, William Atkinson married Lucy Barnes. Writer failed to discover if Mary Bell was the widow of John Bell, or if a relative to Samuel Bell. However, John Bell (1755-1842), Long Glade, Augusta, VA., was listed in the Elizabeth "Betsy" Gilbert family tree.[20]

Hardy Bell (1770-abt. 1866) was Head of (5) Household Members. Grady Locklear's resource states that Hardy Bell was born (1770). According to the Robeson County Deeds, Hardy began to purchase property in 1819. In Land Grant Entry #71, dated 24 Nov 1831, Hardy Bell purchased (10) acres of land situated near the Stage Road. [The Stage Road ran from South Carolina to Fayetteville, NC.] The Land Deed was sealed 29 May 1832. Hardy Bell's death date was discovered in his Last Will and Testament at the Robeson County

[20] Sampson County Deed Book 6 Feb 1804, p. 88.

Courthouse Land Deeds. His land division was between the following children: Amos, Wiley, Semore "Cemore" (1837), and Mary Eliza Bell Smith (1825-1892).

On 10 Apr 1873, the Probate Will of Hardy H. Bell was read to his family members at the Robeson County Courthouse, Lumberton by S. B. Rozier, administrator for the Hardy Bell's estate. [ADDRESS FOR PRIVATE USE]

Seymour [Semore] Bell (1835) married Elizer Hammonds (1850), 30 Mar 1854. Their son was Ervin Hammonds (1853/1855-1930). Ervin married Elizabeth "Betty" Hunt (1859-1914), the daughter of Lewis Hunt. An elder member of the family, Caswell Hunt lived with writer's maternal great-aunt, Mary Eliza Brooks and her husband, Alec Chesley Locklear near the St. Annah Freewill Baptist Church, Pembroke, NC.

Lewis Hunt, Sr., and Mary Polly Oxendine were ancestors of writer's maternal great-grandmother Effie Jane Hunt who married Alexander "Sandy" Brooks, the maternal grandson of Pvt. John Brooks and Pattie, the daughter of Revolutionary War soldier, Pvt. William [Loughery] Lowrie and Elizabeth "Bettie" Locklear, the daughter of Revolutionary War soldier, Pvt. Benet Localare, Warren County, NC.

Ervin and Betty's children: William Jasper, Pauline, and Sophronia, who married Luther Paul. Pauline married William Norman McLean, the son of Sylvester Oxendine McLean. Sylvester was a sister to Ollin Oxendine and Eliza Oxendine Goins. Apparently, another son, Levi McDonald Hammonds was absent when the census enumerator visited Ervin and Betty's home.

Writer discovered Levi McDonald Hammonds (NC, 27 Nov 1884-6 May 1975, PA) married Ella N. Hunt (NC, 1886-1973, PA), 1901. Ella parents were: Ollen Washington Hunt (NC, 11 Sep 1860-9 Dec 1938, SC) and Charity Lorie Oxendine (12 May 1869-14 Oct 1940), 1884. Charity Lorie's parents were: Angus Oxendine and Elizabeth "Edie" Paul.[21]

In the 1850 census, Hardy Bell (age 60) and Sarah "Sally" Bell (age 50), were listed in the same dwelling.

---

[21] Cummings-Woriax, *Creation*, pp. 221, 225 & 283.

Correction: According to Hardy Bell's Sampson County birthdate and according to the 1850 census, his birthdate would be abt. 1790. In addition, Hardy's Bell's grave marker which reads, (H.H. Bell Died Apr 28, 1866, age 80 Yrs, Gone but not forgotten).

Evidence: In 1850, Hardy Bell (1790, age 60), was listed as a merchant, born in Sampson County. Nancy (abt. 1780, age 70), birth place not answered, and Sally Goddin (1824, age 26). No doubt, the Nancy listed was Nancy Carter, the widow of Samuel Bell. In the 1860 tax list, the value of Hardy H. Bell's real estate was valued at $7,000.

According to Mary C. Norment's book, *The Lowrie History*, on pp. 28-29, she wrote that the Bell merchandise store was a burlesque.

Researching the Robeson County census, writer discovered Sally Goddin or Goodin (23) living with Orra Hammonds (40). The following surnames, Goddin [Godwin], Epp's, and Drew, were Indian names discovered in Halifax surnames.

Sally Goddin was Sally "Coartly" Jarvis Goodwin (18 Aug 1818-6 May 1891). She married Jesse P. Goodwin (28 Jun 1802-14 Sep 1880). Jesse P. was the son of Thomas P. Goodwin from Cedar Island, Carteret County, NC. Sally "Coartly Jarvis Goodwin was buried in the Daniels Goodwin Family Cemetery, Carteret County, NC.

Also, writer discovered Godwin, William Burney (1841-16 Jun 1896), served in the Civil War through Company C., 50 North Carolina Infantry. His parents were: W. B. Godwin. William Burney married Sally McLamb/ Lamb, who writer believes is the Sally Goddin above. Perhaps, the following person, Berry Godwin (1859) no doubt, was a relative or a son to the William Burney Godwin. More research is required.

According to the 1860 census, the following were members of the Hardy Bell's household: Hardy (age 74); Sarra [Sarah], (age 60); Amos (age 22); W. (age 17); Westly (age 15); Clarissa (age 12); and, Faney [Fannie] Smith (age 80). Amos Bell (8 May 1837-8 Feb 1919) married Catherine Revels (1844-1924), the daughter of Elijah or Elisha Revels, and Susan Carter. Amos and Catherine's son, Seymour (12 Aug 1875-22 Nov 1957) married Lummie.

Seymour [Seamore] Bell and Mary Hammond were the parents of Helen Bell. Helen Bell (1828-29 Oct 1913) married William Santee, the son of Caesar [Sesar] Santee, a Revolutionary War soldier from Halifax, who served under Capt. Hall's [Heil's] Co. He served under Eaton, 22 Feb 1777. He was taken prisoner of war (POW), 1 Jun 1779; Cesar was discharged in 1781.

Santee, Sesar, served under Capt. Cline Heil, for three years. He lived in Bladen and Robeson County, NC. No doubt, it is possible that his son was William Kennedy Santee (abt. 1816-2 Apr 1853). William Kennedy alias William Canady (1825) is often written as William James Kennedy/Canady (1824-1885). William Santee was the son of Mary S. Santee, Bladen County. His son was William James "Jim" (13 Apr 1853-13 Apr 1933). While researching Duplin County census writer discovered a James Kenady [Canady], (1789) living in Duplin County, NC, in 1850.

Wiley Daniel "Willie" Bell's (31 Aug 1831-1913/1933) parents were: Hardy "Hardie" Bell (1786/1790-29 Apr 1866) and Narcissus "Sis" Hammonds. Hardy's children were: Harriett Bell (1827-10 Nov 1892), Helen Bell (1828-1913), and Amos Bell (1837-8 Feb 1919), who married Catherine Revels (1844-1924).

Wiley "Willie" Bell (15 Mar 1887) married Martha Ann Conner (22 Jun 1828-20 Jan 1910), bondsman: Hardy H. Bell. Wiley and Martha's son, Rev. John J. Bell (22 Jun 1861-24 Dec 1930) married Serena Carter (4 Mar 1859-3 Jun 1929), 24 Aug 1879. Serena parents were: David Carter and Caroline Smith, a sister to David and William Nelson Carter. Martha Ann's parents were: John B. Conner (1803) and Sophia "Sofia" Bledsole (1814) married 7 Feb 1829.

Nelson Carter married Roma Smith, 1832.

Rev. John and Serena's daughter was Winnie Lee Bell. She and Ruth Sampson, the daughter of Oscar Sampson (17 Jan 1866-9 Jan 1928/1978) and Susie Jane Oxendine, were recognized as the first two Indian women to earn a four-year diploma from the early Normal School, Pembroke, NC, now known as the University of North Carolina at Pembroke. Ruth attended the Carson College, TN. Winnie Lee married [George] Josiah Jenkins, who served in the US Navy, WWI. Winnie Lee and her family lived in and at death, she was buried in Iron Mountain, MI.

John B. Conner, a store clerk in the Bell's Merchandise Store, Fourth Street, Lumberton, NC, entered Robeson County from Jones County, NC. Wiley and Martha's daughter, Mattie Rea (16 Jun 1866-16 Jul 1930) married JD Chavis. Mattie Rea married her second husband, Rev. Thaddeus "T. H." Hammons (16 Jun 1866-16 Jul 1938), 5 Jan 1888. Mattie Rea's son was Lumbee Chavis born abt. 1885.

While researching for the Chavis family members in Wake County, NC census, this writer discovered Savannah Holmes (1886) living with Prof. JD and Mattie Chavis. JD [John] Chavis and Savannah Holmes were later listed as teachers in Greensboro, NC.

Thaddeus' parents lived in Sampson County. They were: William Hammonds (1832-1925) and Susan "Susie" Carter (1831-1898) married 25 Dec 1858. Susan "Susie" was the daughter of John S. Carter and Catheran.

William Hammonds was the son of Olin [Ollen] Hammonds and Sylvia "Silvy" Roberts. William married Sallie Jane Jones.

Reading the May 31, 1880, Robeson County Mortality List, writer discovered "Silvy" Hammond, died Sep, (age 64). Sylvania "Silva" Roberts (1815-Sep 1879) married Ollen Hammonds alias Willis Hammons.

In the 13 July 1860 Robeson County census, p. 53, line 1, dwelling #387, family #387, writer discovered Sophia "Sofia" Bledsole Conner (age 36), Winnie (age 22), Harriet (age 20), Ike B. (age 12), and Leander (age 10). Ike B. and Leander were attending school. Writer discovered John Conner living in other states. Writer failed to discover if he was the same John Conner who married Sofia Bledsole Conner.

In dwelling #388 lived Cripsy Conner and in dwelling #389 lived Joshua Shepherd (1831). Joshua married Sarah A. Nye. Could he be the son of Unity [Emily] Shepherd who married William C. Sanderson, 5 Jan 1844? William Sanderson married Sarah A. Oxendine (1834), whose parents were: Esther Lowrie and Jordan Oxendine, married on 12 Mar 1835.

Jordan Oxendine was a witness to Susan Locklier in her disposition for William Loughry [Lowrie] Revolutionary War pension. William (1750/1758-

26 May 1847, age 97) was the son of elder James Lowrie. Could Esther Lowrie be the daughter of Susan Locklier and William Loughry? William Loughry [Lowrie] was this writer's (6x) maternal great-grandfather.

Wiley Bell and Martha Ann Conner's daughter, Sarah C. Bell (1859-1933) married James W. Blanks (12 Apr 1847-27 Jan 1912). Their children were: Docia (1872), John (1874), and Ella (1879).

James W. Blanks married Sarah C. Bell, a descend of Revolutionary War soldier, Samuel Bell. Rev. James Blanks became a clergyperson in the early Burnt Swamp Baptist Association in 1881. The Association name was changed to The Burnt Swamp Baptist Association of the Mixed Race and in 1885, the name was changed to The Burnt Swamp Association of the Croatan Race. Today, the Association is known as the Burnt Swamp Baptist Association and now holds a membership within the NC Baptist Conference and the National Southern Baptist Association. [ADDRESS FOR PRIVATE USE]

The Rev. Cary Wilkins served as the first Moderator to the newly formed Indian Association, 21 Jan 1881. In her Doctoral Project, this writer wrote that Cary Wilkins was greatly involved in both political and religious arenas during the unrest and injustices in Robeson County. Rev. Furney Prevatte, former Confederate soldier, assisted Rev. Wilkins in both political and religious issues in the Indian communities.

Rev. Wilkins was elected to serve as a Chief Administrator during the Homestead Act in 1860. Cary served as a land surveyor; an appraiser of property; Justice of the Peace; and elected town registrar at St. Pauls, NC. [ADDRESS FOR PRIVATE USE]

Blanks, James W., Pvt., served in the Civil War through NC Company F, 51st Infantry Regiment. He was wounded in the shoulder at Ft. Drewry [Drury] Bluff, VA, 15 May 1862. The fort is also known as Fort Darling.

The Battle at Ft. Drewry was given the name in honor of Captain (Capt.) August H. Drewry. The fort sat on his private property on a 90-ft bluff. The fort's fortifications housed large guns.[22]

---

[22] Cummings-Woriax, *American Indian Patriots*, p. 105.

James Blanks was hospitalized in Richmond, VA. At his death, he was buried in the Ten Mile Center Baptist Church Cemetery, Lumberton, NC.

Could James Blanks' mother be Amelia "Emily" Blanks (1825)? Amelia married Elias Revels (1765-22 Nov 1806), 16 Mar 1844, Robeson County. Emily formerly lived in Pilot, Surry County, NC.

Hardy "Hardie" Bell married Allen [Alean or Alene] Hammonds, 1836, Robeson County. Nelson Smith was a witness. Nelson Smith (1820-1880) married Eliza Bell (1825), 14 Dec 1836, the daughter of Hardy Bell (1770) and Sarah Parker (1800). Nelson Smith was the guardian of Clarissa Revels according to the Hardy Bell's estate settlement, 18 Feb 1873.

William Nelson Carter married Helen Revels (1837-1912), 24 Nov 1855. His mother was Bethania [Locklear], (1790), Brunswick County, NC. Nelson Carter married Roma Smith, 1832.

According to the U.S. Federal Census Mortality Schedule, 1850-1885 for N.W. Smith, (d. age 59), p. 2, year ending May 1880, Robeson County, submitted by recorder, B. McLean.[23] However, Nelson "N.W." Smith died Nov 1879.

Evidence: Nelson [N. W.] Smith was born in 1820, not 1837, according to the 1850 Mortality List and his children's date of birth.

Nelson and Eliza's daughter, Caroline "Catlin" (10 Mar 1838-2 Feb 1920) married David Carter (1834-24 Jan 1912), 29 Nov 1856. Their son, Alonza "Lonzy" Carter (10 Sep 1876-13 Oct 1960) married Rhodicy Wilkins (28 Feb 1884-9 Nov 1922). Sion Wilkins (5 Sep 1786-1880) and Rhodicy "Dicey" Carter (1787-1880) were the parents of Rev. Cary Wilkins (1826). Rev. Cary Wilkins married Sarah Revels (1822), 13 Oct 1855. [ADDRESS FOR PRIVATE USE]

Alonza and Rhodicy's daughter, Serena "Rena" Carter (4 Mar 1859-3 Jun 1929) married John J. Bell (22 Jun 1861-24 Dec 1930), 24 Aug 1879. John J. Bell was the son of Wiley Bell (31 Aug 1831-9 Apr 1909) and Martha Ann Conners (22 Jun 1828-20 Jan 1910), 8 Mar 1854. Rev. John J. Bell and Serena "Rena Lee" Carter lived in St. Pauls, NC. Both were buried in the Bell Cemetery, near Magnolia School, Lumberton, NC.

---

[23] US Federal Census Morality Schedule, 1850-1885, p. 2.

David and Caroline's children: Margaret (May 1854-29 Dec 1914) married Miles Henry Godwin; Serenah [Serena] married John J. Bell; Nelson; Isabella married Cain Chavis, 12 Dec 1882; Alonzo [Lansey/Lonzy] married Rhodicy Wilkins; his second wife, Odee "O.D." Locklear Chavis (4 Oct 1890-2 Feb 1973) was the widow of John Chavis, married 3 Jul 1903; William Henry married Beulah Carter; Fannie (20 Apr 1858-18 Jun 1918) married Walter Steel Wilkins; Sarah Eliza married Malcolm Carter; Alvin "Alva" married Minnie Goins; Will married Mary Ann Chavis; Daniel married Manervia Smith Carter; Lula; Mary Susan; and, Floyd, who died in FL.

Miles Henry Godwin's parents were: Quincey Godwin and Sally Sarah Hammonds (1827-1926). Miles Henry and Margaret lived in Wakulla, FL. Quincy Godwin married Carrie Mae Emanuel (18 Dec 1900-19 May 1975), lived in FL the same year.

Grady Locklear writes, Isabella and Cain Chavis were living in Santa Rosa County, FL in 1915, while, Sara Eliza and Malcolm Carter resided in Covington County, AL.

Minnie Goins married Edmund [Alvin] Carter, 28 Dec 1899, Forsyth County, NC. Minnie's parents were: Joe and Mary Goins. At Minnie and Edmund's marriage, her father Joe, was living and her mother, Mary, was deceased.

Fannie Carter Wilkins burned to death when her clothing caught fire at the family outdoor wash pot. Grady Locklear's resource suggests that Fannie Carter Smith was buried on the Georgia side of the St. John's River and her brother, Floyd, was buried on the opposite side of the St. John's River in Florida.

Carter, Daniel [David], (abt. 1830-Apr 1892), Pvt., served in the Civil War through Company C., NC 54th Infantry Regiment, Cumberland County, NC. He was a Confederacy prisoner of war (POW). His parents were: Josiah Carter (1800-May 1870) and Katherine Purcell (1808), Dismal Swamp, Sampson County, NC. David Carter married Lucy C. Horne (1842), 21 Feb 1859, Cumberland County, NC.

Lucy C. Horne married William S. Hall, 3 Apr 1894. William S. [Schoofield] Hall (1837), Little Coharie, Sampson County, entered the Civil War, 9 May 1861, through Company F, NC 20th Infantry Regiment.[24]

---

[24] Cummings-Woriax, *American Indian Patriots*, p. 109.

Carter, Josiah, Sr., (1762-24 Jun 1835), Pvt., W8187, served in the Revolutionary War in the NC Continental-Line. He married Betsy Doggett. After his death in 1832, (age 72), his pension was $33, which commenced 1 Apr 1833. His pension was awarded to his widow, Mary Brock, presumably his widow's maiden name, or Josiah's second wife.

Carter, Josiah, Jr., (1797/1800- May 1870), served in the Civil War as a Confederate soldier through Sampson County, NC. He married Mary Ham [Horne], 13 Dec 1866. According to his pension record his widow, Mary Ham Carter received his pension. The U.S. Federal Census Mortality Schedules, Sampson County, NC, list Josiah Carter's death, May 1870.[25]

Grady Locklear's resource suggests that William Carter and David Carter's father, William Nelson Carter drew up his Last Will & Testament, 8 May 1842, Cumberland County, NC. He left his five children and property to Corporal Peter Port. Grady Locklear suggest that William Nelson's death was 1842.

In the 1850 Cumberland County census writer discovered William Carter and David Carter were living with Jesse and Elizabeth Burnet [Burnette] in dwelling #613 and family #626, line #5, western division, 28 Aug 1850. The census lists both boys, William (age 16) and David (age 14) years-of-age. However, on pages 51 and 52 in the Grady Locklear resource, he writes that William was (16) sixteen years-of-age and David was (14) fourteen years-of-age at the time of their father's death in 1842. [ADDRESS FOR PRIVATE USE]

Jesse and Elizabeth Burnet's son, Needham [Rany] Burnet (1830) married Nancy Parker, 2 May 1833. Needham married Caroline Hagins, 11 Oct 1855, Robeson County.

An older Needham Burnett (1813) married Nancy Gay. Malcolm Burnett's parents were: Samuel and Nancy Burnett. At her death, Nancy was listed as Ceila Lucas.

David Burnett married Delphia Hammonds, 13 Nov 1860, whose parents were: Owen and Docia Hammonds Revels. Bondsman, Henry Parker. Henry

---

[25] The U.S. Federal Census Mortality Schedules, 1850-1885, Sampson County, NC, ancestry.com accessed:

Parker married Polly Bell, Sampson County, 9 Sep 1824, in Robeson County. Hardy Bell was a witness to their marriage.

Jesse Parker married Susan Jackson, 9 Aug 1838. Ollen Hammonds and Ishmale [Ishmeal] Roberts were witnesses. Perhaps, Nancy Parker, Jesse Parker, and Henry Parker were relatives.

Neil Burnett married Katie Bell Hagans (18 Apr 1894), whose parents were: John Henry Hagans (19 Nov 1854-30 Aug 1933) and Annie Jane (2 Sep 1860-11 Oct 1931). Katie's sister, Fannie Hagans (1889-1980) married John Walter Hardin (11 Sep 1879-12 Oct 1965).

James Hagen (9 Jul 1879-8 Dec 1961) married Lener Bell (1883-11 Jun 1914), whose parents were: Wily Bell and Martha Ann Conners.

Port, Peter (1750), Corporal, served in the Revolutionary War. In 1790, he lived in Bladen County. In 1820, Peter Port married June Carter, 9 May 1820, Cumberland County, NC. In 1820, Peter Port and his family lived in Pee Dee, Georgetown, SC. Peter Port was enumerated 7 August 1820, SC. In 1840, he lived in Fayetteville, NC. Following David Carter death, Peter Port provided care and served as executor of the Carter's property, Cumberland County, NC. [ADDRESS FOR PRIVATE USE]

David Carter married Caroline Smith, 29 Nov 1856. Writers have stated that she lived to be (104) years-of-age. However, according to her NC Death Certificate, Caroline Smith was (96) years-of-age.

David and Caroline's son, John Samuel Bell (18 Dec 1888-29 Jan 1957) married Zelma Wiley (31 Mar 1899-8 May 1979). John Samuel was listed as a merchant. He was killed in an auto/truck collision, Maxton, NC. Both, he and Zelma were buried in the Magnolia Cemetery, Harlesville [Little Rock], SC.

Alvin A. Carter's parents were: Daniel [David] Carter and Caroline Smith, married 29 Nov 1856. Alvin A. Carter married Minnie E. Goins.

Daniel David Carter's parents were: William Nelson Smith and Eliza Bell. Daniel David married Mary Ray, 29 Sep 1859. Also, he married Minerva Jane Smith.

Pvt. Golden Andrew Carter (11 Dec 1901-4 Jun 1976), served in the US Army, WWII. His parents were: Alvin A. Carter and Minnie E. Goins. Golden Andrew Carter married Ila Thelma Smith (1903), 27 Feb 1921. Golden Andrew Carter and Ila Thelma Smith Carter were buried in the Carter Cemetery, Red Springs, NC.

Ila Thelma Smith's parents were: Charles H. and Frances Smith. Witnesses were: N. M. Carter and Henry Hammonds. The Rev. W. A. Bell officiated.

Golden and Ila Thelma's son, Pvt. Golden Lester Carter, Jr., (17 Aug 1922-22 May 1959), served in the US Army, WWII. Golden Lester married Lucille Grove. Her parents were: Claude and Annie Grove, Averasboro, Harnett County, NC. Golden Lester was buried in the Sycamore Hill Freewill Baptist Church, Maxton, NC.

Millie [Brayboy] Hammonds, the daughter of John [David] and Lydia Brayboy, married Tom Sampson, the son of elder Henry Sampson. In 1850, Milly (abt. 1767, age 83), was living in the home of her son, Henry [II] and Nancy Hammond, Cumberland County, NC. Henry [II] was also known as Henry Sampson.

Thomas Sampson Land Deed Transactions:

On 5 Mar 1819, Thomas Sampson purchased 100 acres from Elisha Cumbo. According to Robeson County Deed Book T, p. 9, date, 17 June 1820, a land transaction between Marmaduke Etheridge who sold 3 tracts of land to Thomas Sampson. In 1825, per Deed Book X, p. 522, Thomas Sampson willed land to his son, Henry Sampson. Rachel Carter, who was Thomas Sampson's second wife and the stepmother to Henry Sampson (II). She filed for her dowry from her husband's, Thomas Sampson estate. According to the November term 1839, Court of Pleas and Quarter, November term 1839, shows that Rachel Carter filed suit against Henry

Sampson. According to the 1840 May Term, Rachel Carter won her suit. However, her interest in the estate was auction off to the highest bidder which was Henry Sampson.

Lastly, in Deed Book BB, p. 119, on 3 Sep 1951 Sixth, Register of Deeds, Book BB, p. 119, on 3 Sep 1951, Henry Sampson purchased a tract of land from Elizabeth Sampson. The above is evidence that Henry Sampson was born and reared in Robeson County.[26]

According to his war pension information, Thomas became an invalid 30 Apr 1885 and died before 1899. Rachel Sampson's widow's pension began 15 Jun 1899, Maryland.

Rachel Chavers/Chavis Sampson married James Carter, 17 Mar 1830, Robeson County, NC.

Rachel and James Carter's son was Richard Carter. Rachel sought her Dower Feb 1840. Their daughter, Elizabeth's guardian was her brother, Henry Sampson. Henry's son was Thomas Sampson.

In the 1850 census, Richard Carter (age 18), Helen (age 20), Rachel Carter (age 40), Mary J. Oxendine (age 18), Joe (age 19), Orra (age 14), and Hulda (age 8), lived in Robson County.

Henry Sampson who married Nancy Carter (20 Dec 1802-18 Nov 1897), lived in the Deep Branch Community. His parents were: Milly Brayboy and Thomas Sampson. Milly's parents were: John [David] and Lydia Brayboy. Milly [Brayboy] Hammonds, age eighty-three (83, abt. 1767), was living in the Sampson household in Cumberland County, NC.

Carter, Henry, served in the Revolutionary War. He married Sarah Carter, Nov 1821. Henry Carter lived in Sampson County in 1800 as Head of (8) Household Members. Henry Carter died 25 Dec 1848. Sarah Carter made application for his pension in 1848. Apparently, he and Sarah were the parents of (6) children.

---

[26] Cummings-Brooks, *Creation*, pp. 190.

Henry Carter, Jr., (1812-1879) married Queenie Elizabeth Horne (1827-1889), 10 Oct 1845, Cumberland County.

Henry's second wife was: Molsey [Monzey] Johnson (1853), 25 Feb 1876. Could she have been Molsy Wilkins living in Duplin County, NC, 1850? Henry and Queenie's children were: Mary Carter (May 1867-1933) and Daniel Carter (13 Jun 1871-20 Apr 1937).

Carter, Henry (abt. 1815-1879, military date), Pvt., Cumberland County, served in the Confederate Army, through the 43rd NC Regiment Infantry, 20 Apr 1862. Henry married Mary (NKA).

Henry and Mary's children were: Benjamin Roberson who married Henrietta. He served in the US Army, WWI. David Neil married Martha Jane; Elizabeth married William James Canady; Daniel; James Washington; William Francis; Margaret A.; and, Catherine Carter.

Carter, Neil, whose parents were: Robert and Martha Carter. No doubt, Neil Carter was a relative to Calvin Christian Carter, listed below. Neil served in Company E, 51st NC Infantry Regiment. He was wounded in the war. At his death, he was buried in the Long Branch Baptist Church Cemetery.

Carter, Calvin Christian (Jan 1835-12 Jun 1917), Pvt., served in the Confederacy War in the 31st Infantry A-D. Calvin married Frances Carter (Jan 1845-Jan 1912). Calvin's father was: Luke Carter who married Susan Thompson. Luke Carter also married Eliza N. Carter. Luke Carter (1796) married Elizabeth Carter.

Grady Locklear write that Henry Carter married Orilla Carter. In 1914, the couple were living in Marion, SC. Henry Carter later married Sarah McLamb/Lamb, the former spouse of Peter Lamb.

In this writer's book, *Patriots Soldiers*, Zechariah Carter (11 Apr 1824-5 Sep 1888) married Elizabeth McLamb/Lamb, 28 Dec 1844. Pvt., Carter served in the Civil War, Company E, North Carolina 51st Infantry Regiment. He enlisted 28 Feb 1862; entered 10 Apr 1862. Following the war, Zachariah became a clergyperson. Zechariah Carter was buried in the Rice Cemetery, Britt Township, Lumberton, NC.

Carter, Sr., Henry, Pvt., served in the Revolutionary War. He married Sarah Carter, Nov 1821. He lived in Sampson County in 1800 as Head of (8) Household Members. Sarah Carter made application for his war pension in 1848. Henry Carter died, 25 Dec 1848. Apparently, he and Sarah were the parents of (6) children.

Barnes, Willis (1832), Pvt., served in the Civil War through Co. B, NC 5th Regiment Infantry, 5 1862. Willis was promoted to Sgt., 11 Jul 1862, then promoted to Full Lt. His parents were: Hardy and Mary J. Ivey Barnes. He married Mary Ella Regan (24 Jun 1856), 9 May 1872. Mary Ella Regan's parents were: Jonathan Wishart Regan and Rhoda Caldwell.

Mary J. Ivey, no doubt, was a descendant of Thomas and Elizabeth Ivey's family who were living in the Saddletree Community in 1761. Mary Ella Regan's father, Jonathan Wishart Regan, was a descendant of Capt. Regan of the Captain Regan's District. Thomas Ivey was issued a Land Grant, 26 Nov 1789.

See author Hicks' article below:

> Thomas Hagan, Thomas Ivey and his wife, Elizabeth Ivey, and their daughter, Kesiah Ivey, appeared in the Marion County, SC Court of Common Pleas, October Term 1812 regarding levy [taxes] placed upon all Free Negros Mulatoes. Robert Coleman stated that he was acquainted with Thomas and Elizabeth for abt. eight to nine years. He commented Thomas was of Portuguese descent and his wife was white.
>
> Their daughter Kesiah Ivey married Zachariah Hagans. John Regan testified that he had known the Ivey's for abt. twelve to fifteen years…. that the family lived near Drowning Creek, Bladen County [Robeson County], NC.
>
> In the 1780 census, Thomas Ivey lived in the Fayette [Fayetteville] District, Robeson County as Head of (11) Household Members.[27]

---

[27] Hicks, Theresa, *South Carolina Indians Indian traders and Other Ethnic Connections Beginning in 1670*, pp. 298-299.

Mary Regan (1832) married Thomas Willis (1839), 18 Mar 1873. While reading early 1753 Land Deeds, writer discovered Benjamin, David, and John Willis living in the Saddletree Community. The Willis' ancestors, Joseph Willis and Ageton Willis, entered into New Hanover and Bladen County from Isle of Wright, VA.

A younger, Mary Ella Regan (29 Aug 1899-4 Jul 1960) married Herman Thompson. Mary Ella's parents were: Joe Neal Regan and Jo Anna Pate.

William Nelson Carter (1834-15 1899) married Hellen [Bell] Revels (1837-8 Mar 1912), 24 Nov 1855. Their children were: William James married Ruth Locklear; Emaline married John Goins; David [Daniel] married Minerva; Malcolm married Sara Eliza Carter (1827); Arrony; Rosella married Benjamin C. Locklear; Queen; Doctor married Mary Goins; Elmira; and, Ashberry.

In 1870, Eliza Carter was listed as a nurse. Others living in her household were: James, Luke, Hughes, and Wesley. Writer discovered Eliza Carter living in Perry, AL in 1880. Other family members were: Bob Carter (1827) and Louisa Carter (1864).

Eliza Carter (35), F, was listed as nurse and cook for the poor house residents in the 1860 US Federal Census p. 115, dwelling #883, family, the Poor House. The residents were: Elisha Branch (82), M, M, [Mulatto]; Martha Branch (9), F; Malachy Thomason (36), F; Emily Thompson, (6), F; Nancy Morgan (58), F; Mary A. Moore (48), F; Rials Shepherd (Unable to determine age if 26 or 96), M; Kiza Gilbert (60), F; and, Josephine Britt, F.[28]

Harriett Bell, the daughter of Wiley and Martha Ann Conner Bell (1800) married Dolphus Harden or Hardin or Harding (1820). Their son, Condary Hardin (1851-1931) married Amarett Hammonds (1863-1928), whose daughter was Nasba (1879).

In the 1850 Robeson County census, Thomas Carter was living in the household of Pasty Carter (1803) with Alexander Carter (1822). In the 1860 census, Thomas was living in the Martha Carter's household, Robeson County, NC. Martha Carter was Head of (12) Household Members: Alice (1825); Ora

[28] Adapted from 1860 US Federal Census, p. 115, ancestry.com accessed: 20 Aug 2016.

[Orra], (1831); Catherine/Catharine (1841); Thomas (1839); Alexander (1840); Charity (1842); Noah (1844); Delila [Lila], (1849); John (1858); Leonora (1857); and, William (age 10/12 months).

Carter, Thomas (abt. 1839), Robeson County, served in the Civil War through the 5th NC Infantry Company, A. On 5 May 1862, Thomas was killed in action (KIA) in the Battle of Williamsburg, VA. He entered 4 May 1861. Thomas was buried in the Cedar Grove Cemetery, Williamsburg, VA.[29]

In the Robeson County 1850 census, writer discovered Sarah Parker (abt. 1800), (50) years-of-age, living with Patsey Woodal [Woodle or Martha Patsy Woodell], William Hammons, Angus Harden [Hardin], Michael Smith (age 45), Willie [Wiley] Bell (age 18), Helen Bell (age 22), Simon Bell (age 14), and Amos Bell (age 13) were living in dwelling #322, family #322.

Michael Smith was listed as a tailor. Perhaps, he worked as a tailor in the Bells Merchandise store in Lumberton. Michael Smith emigrated to America from Ireland, Great Britain.

Nancy Woodell's (1867-27 Oct 1920) parents were: Solomon Oxendine (1832-1897) and Martha Patsy Woodell (1832-9 Dec 1879/1880). Martha Patsy's parents were: Martin [Marten] Woodell (abt. 1803-1852) and Rosada Spivey Israel, the daughter of Matthew and Gracy Spivey, Montgomery County, NC. Rosada was the former wife of John Israel, a Civil War soldier. Israel was also written as Ezzell.

Jerry Woodell's parents were: Marden Woodell and Mary Duckery (abt. 1800-1852), Guilford County, NC. Marden's [Martin] parents were: Jerry Woodall (German) and Mary Polly Pravatt/ Prevatte (Scotch).

Jeremiah "Jerry" Woodell (abt. 1825) married Rhodie [Rhoda] Britt (1822), whose parents were: Jesse Britt and Lechie Burns. It is stated that Jesse Britt's skin was light; hair long and coarse; and black eyes.

Could Mary Polly Prevatt/e (abt. 1846) be a relative to Furney Prevatt, Sr? His son was Rev. Furney Prevatt, Jr., who married Isabella Currie. One of their daughters was given the name Polly [Molly] Prevatt. She married James Conley,

---

[29] Cummings-Woriax, *American Indian Patriots*, p. 116.

Lumber Bridge, NC. Another daughter, Lula P. [Isabella Frances] Prevatt (1870) married Rev. John Lee Humphrey (1871). He died and was buried in TX. Lula was buried in the Saddletree Christian Cemetery, Lumberton, NC. Other Prevatt/e family members were buried in the Prevatte Cemetery, Lumberton, NC.

In the 1880 Robeson County census, writer discovered Martin Woodell living as a resident in the poor house. He was (age 72) and blind.

Solomon Oxendine's parents were: William "Billy" Oxendine (abt. 1800-1875) and Susan Revels (1845-1870), 10 Jan 1861. Martha Patsy Woodell's second husband was James Brayboy. Their son was George Brayboy.

Solomon Oxendine (abt. 1833-4 Jan 1897) married Flora Jane Ransome Chavis (abt. 1864), 10 Jan 1884. Flora Jane's parents were: Henry and Anna Chavis. Solomon was buried in the Oxendine Cemetery.

Martha Patsy Woodell and Solomon Oxendine's children:

Alonza H. (1854-1946); Daniel Webster "Webb" (1857); Joseph W. (1861); Elias; Martha Jane; Amanda F.; Melissa; Nancy; and, William. Alonza H. Oxendine married Nancy Charity Oxendine (1860-1935) or Charity Oxendine Jacobs (13 Feb 1851-6 Jan 1934).

Daniel Webb Oxendine married Christine Oxendine, whose parents were: Archibald and Margaret "Peggie" Oxendine (1835-1914). Their daughters were: Josephine and Mary Margaret. Josephine married Willie Henry Emanuel, Bulloch, GA. Mary Margaret Oxendine married Reasley Cummings, the son of Virginia Cummings, the daughter of Eliza Swett Cummings. It has been suggested that Virginia's father was Dave Strickland. Reasley and Margaret lived in Bulloch, GA.

According to writer's book, *Creation*, Dave Strickland was a relative to Joel Strickland's (16 Oct 1837-1867), whose parents were Ellender Strickland (1790) and Alexander Strickland. His sister, Maria (1821) married Samuel Sweet/Sweat, the son of Nathan Sweat in Ware, GA, 1850.

Grover C. Woodell's (GA, 18 Apr 1893-1 Mar 1931, NC) parents were: James Amos Woodell and Nancy Ann Oxendine. Grover C. Woodell served in the US Army WWI, in the 344th, F. A. Battalion B. Grover married Mary

France Baker (1897-1958), 7 Dec 1919. Grover and Mary Frances were buried in the Oxendine Cemetery, Pembroke, NC.

John Edmond Woodell's (16 Dec 1884-23 Oct 1946) parents were: James Amos Woodell and Nancy Oxendine. He married Minnie Sanderson, the daughter of Travis Sanderson and Martha Oxendine.

According to Robert Garfield Woodell's (21 Jan 1889-3 Feb 1968), WWI military draft card, his parents were: James Amos Woodell and Nancy Oxendine. Robert claimed the following exemption: his mother, Nancy Oxendine Woodell was deaf and dumb. Robert himself also experienced hearing and speaking difficulties. Robert Woodell never married.

James Von Woodell's (3 Aug 1887-5 Oct 1981) parents were: James Amos and Nancy Oxendine Woodell. James Von married Ella Florence Smith. Their son, Clayton Harmon Woodell (NC, 6 Mar 1916-Oct 1976, VA), served in the US Army, WWII. Apparently, Clayton was reared by his paternal grand-parents: James Amos and Nancy Ann Oxendine Woodell.

Braddy Brantley Woodell's (24 Jan 1901-4 Feb 1993) parents were: James Amos and Nancy Oxendine Woodell. Braddy married Carlee [Carrie Lee] Locklear, whose parents were: Samp (28 Jan 1874-26 Dec 1955) and Gatsy Locklear (1 May 1870-23 Feb 1939). Samp's mother was Effy Ann Locklear.

Braddy's second marriage was to Myrtle Locklear, the daughter of John Bunyan Locklear and Downie Chavis, whose parents were: Benjamin Franklin and Mackealy Chavis (1864-30 Jan 1930). Mackealy's parents were: William Chavis and Queenie Maynor.

Pvt. John Bunyan Locklear served in the US Army, WWI. His parents were: Samp and Gatsy Locklear. He married Dovie Chavis, the daughter of Mackealy Chavis. Pvt. Bunyan and his family lived next to writer's paternal aunt Lillian Cumming and Chester Oxendine in the Harpers Ferry Community.

Martha Patsy Woodell Carter married Rufus [Johnson] Woodell (1854). Rufus married Eliza J. Oxendine, 11 Sep 1875. Their twin babies, Claude and Shandy, were listed as only 8/12 months- of-age. Rufus' parents were: Jeremiah and Rody Woodell. He married Mary McLaughlin (1847), 6 Jun 1878. They lived in Liberty, GA. In 1880, Rufus J. [Johnson] Woodell was appointed as a Postmaster in Wayne County, GA. After Mary's death, Rufus lived with his brother, Mark Woodell, in FL.

Rufus Woodell's (23 Jan 1873-2 Jan 1944, military date), parents were: Jeremiah and Rody Woodell. Prior to his enlistment in the US Army, WWII, Rufus lived with his stepmother, Eliza Carter, Robeson County, NC. Rufus married Mary McLaughlin, 6 Jun 1878, Liberty, GA.

Another Rufus W. [Lowry] Woodell (1854) was listed living among the Lowries in the Hopewell Community. He married Burro [Burough] Lowry (20 Jun 1871-8 Aug 1964), whose parents were: Rev. Calvin Calhoun Lowry and Maria Sampson, the son of Allen and Polly Cumbo Lowry. Burro died in Highland Park, MD. She was buried in Elizabeth City, NC.

Rev. Rufus W. [Lowry] Woodell was appointed to the Bethel [Dogwood] Church as a clergyperson in the Methodist Episcopal Church. In 1905 and in 1909, Rev. W.R. [Rufus] Woodell was admitted to the NC Atlantic Methodist Conference. On 17 Oct 1911, Rev. Woodell was elected and ordained as an Elder in the NC Methodist Church. He was appointed to the Wildwood & Harkers Island Charge off the coast of NC and VA. Later, Rev. Woodell transferred to the Wilmington Conference. [ADDRESS FOR PRIVATE USE]

Continuation: The Pvt. Samuel Bell Family:

Dolphus Harden [Hardin/Harding] and Harriet Bell's children: Daniel Holmes (1845-1920) married Ailey Revels (1849-1926); Amos (1859-7 Apr 1915); Eliza (1861); William (1863); Hellen (1866); and, Molly 1865). Amos Hardin married Annie "Puss" Locklear (1864-13 Jun 1909), whose father was: Anderson Locklear. Amos' son was William Andrew Hardin (1885). Amos' second marriage was to Maulda Locklear (1888), 2 Apr 1910.

Ailey [Alle] Revels' parents were: Elijah Revels and Susan Carter. Alle and Daniel's daughter, Mollie (1875-23 Mar 1950) married Riley Angus Chavis (20 Jun 1860-20 Jun 1925).

Mollie and Riley Angus' children: Tracy, Garfield, and two infants who died at birth.

Daniel Hardin and Ailey Revels were buried in the Stewartsville Cemetery, Scotland County, NC. Their daughter, Louise Hardin married Vance Jones. Vance and Louise were parents of twin daughter, Ella Jones and Alice Jones.

Angus Hayes Harden/Hardin (28 Jun 1868) married Susan Bodiford (7 Jun 1843-15 Apr 1928), 28 Jun 1868. Susan's parents were: Stephen Bodiford and Esther Phillipp.

Orra Bodiford married Israel Campbell, 14 Jan 1837. Their son, Pink Campbell (15 Aug 1855-13 Oct 1941) married Maggie. Perhaps, Orra Bodiford Campbell's mother was Alice Lovett.

Arry Jane Lowry (22 Sep 1882-22 Mar 1966) married William B. Wilkins (4 Feb 1881-11 Jun 1963). Arry Jane's parents were: Neal Archie Lowry and Exey Ann Lowry. William B. was the son of Wellington W. Wilkins and Telatha Lowry.

Arry Jane and Williams' children: Thelma, Laylock (20 Mar 1909-4 Jan 1959), and Welch Wishart Wilkins (1 Aug 1919-11 Nov 1970).

Henry Frank Hardin (27 Aug 1877-16 Jun 1949), whose parents were: Mary Graham and Frederick Hardin. Walden Hardin (11 Sep 1879-12 Oct 1965) married Fannie Hagen (1889-1980). Their daughter, Stella Jane Hardin Locklear Oxendine (1 May 1912-6 Apr 2012) married George Locklear.

In the 1860 census, Hardy Bell was born (abt. 1786). His wife was Sarah (abt. 1800). Hardy and Sarah's children were: Amos (8 May 1838-8 Feb 1919); W. (1843); Westly (1845); Clarissa (1848); and, Faney [Smith], (abt. 1780). Amos married Catherine Revels (1844-1924), 14 Aug 1866. Catherine's parents were: Elijah or Elisha Revels and Susan Carter. Amos and Catherine's children were: Seymour, Rosie, Nancy, and Malendia [Malinda].

Younger Elijah Revels (1813-) married Susan "Sookie" Carter (26 Mar 1823-11 Jun 1895), 30 Dec 1843. Elijah was the son of Edmund Revells. Their son, William "Billy" Revels (1857-1937) married Maggie Locklear. Susan was buried in the Revels-Hammonds Cemetery, Saddletree Community, Lumberton, NC.

Pvt. Elijah Revels served in the Revolutionary War through Sampson County. For his service, he was awarded six hundred and forty acres of land in NC, 30 Sep 1785.

Elijah "Elias" Revels married Dolly [Burden], (1811). Elijah and Dolly's children were: Beda (1780-1855), Rabourn, and Ezekiel.

In the Woriax family history, Beda married Jesse Manuel, Sampson County, NC. The Manuels moved to and at death were buried in Greeneville, Greene County, TN.

Who was Sammey Revels (1830-25 Feb 1894) and Magon Revels (1836-14 Nov 1906)? And, Malcolm and Mary Revels' daughter, Elizabeth (22 Jul 1887-30 Jun 1904). All were buried in the Revels Cemetery, Lumberton, NC. Writer discovered Malcolm Revels' name on his grave marker was written as Magon Revels.

Sammey [Samuel] Revels' (1830-25 Feb 1894) parents were: Owen John Revels (1799/1804-1882) and Dorcas Hammonds (1797) married 23 Apr 1831. Dorcas filed for her dower, 24 Mar 1882. Sammy married Charity Oxendine, 5 Mar 1860. Her father was Solomon Oxendine. Sammy was listed as a widower in the 1880 census. Sammy and Charity's daughter, Mary (5 Mar 1860-15 Jul 1942) married Abner Chavis (16 Jan 1860-16 Jan 1925), 1 Feb 1880.

Mary and Abner Chavis' son, William Roy Chavis (5 May 1902), served in the US Army, WWII.

Malcolm Revels' (d. 4 Nov 1905) parents were: Nathaniel Revels and Mary Elizabeth Lowrie (1771/1785-Aug 1850), 1800. Mary Elizabeth's parents were: progenitor James Lowry and Sarah "Sallie" or "Celia" Kersey. Malcolm married Nancy Deese, the daughter of Murdoch [Murdock] Lowry and Elizabeth Deas [Deese]. Perhaps, another daughter was the Susan Dees who married Agerton Willis, 22 May 1848.

Elizabeth Revels' (22 Jul 1887-30 Jun 1904) parents were: Malcolm and Nancy Revels.

Elias Revels (1765-22 Nov 1806) married Amelia "Emily" Blanks (1825), 16 Mar 1844, Saddletree, Robeson County, NC. Elias and Emily were former residents living in Pilot, Surry County, NC.

Elias and Emily's children were: Henry Snow (1861), Dollie (1864), Mack G. [E.], (1871), and Willis G. (1864), a grandson.

Elijah's third marriage was to Isabella Ann Michel, 7 Mar 1862, Guilford County, NC.

Elias and Dolly's children: Bedea "Beaty," Rabourn, and Ezekial, Nash County, NC, 1775.[30]

Elijah's brother, Micajah Revels (1804-12 Apr 1889) married Nancy "Mourning/Morning Star" Jacobs (1808-27 Feb 1881), 22 Nov 1825, Robeson County, NC. Micajah and Mourning's children were: Henry, Stephen, Aaron, and Rev. John W. Revels (1844-1914). John was Cherokee according to the Dawes Commission Index (1896). However, his application for membership was over-turned by the Dawes Commission in 1896. Further research required.

Micajah and Morning Star's daughter, Mary Jane Delany (1850-13 Aug 1941). Their sons, Aaron, Henry, and John Revels, served in the Civil War as Union soldiers. Henry Revels died from complications suffered from a chronic liver disease which he contracted in the war. Mary Jane was buried in the Revels Cemetery, Wisconsin (WS).

Who was Henry Revels that was murdered, 5 May 1865, Robeson County, NC? In her book, *Creation*, writer discovered one Henry Revels who shot Dr. Daniel Smith, Feb 1872. On 5 May 1865, one Henry Revels [whose complexion was a "Copper color"] was murdered. His skull was fractured. Henry Revels was found in the "Old Field." The Old field was located near Floral McDonald Church. Writer failed to discover family members of both Henry Revels.

Micajah lived in Sampson County, NC in 1810. The Revels family moved to GA in 1860. While living in GA, he married Susan Lee, 1832. The Revels family settled in Wisconsin. The Revels lived in and at death were buried in the Revels Family and the Winchel Family Cemetery, Wisconsin (WS).

Mycajah Revell (1750-1830) married Mary Wadkins. He received a Kentucky Land Grant, 6 Jul 1799 and a General Land Grant in Vernon County, Wisconsin, 24 April 1820.

[30] Cummings-Woriax, *Creation*, p. 545.

Mycajah and Mary's son, Ethelred B. Revelle (1772-1845) was born in Nash County, NC and died in Bollinger, MO. He married Elizabeth Combs. Ethelred assisted in building the first Baptist Association west of the Mississippi.[31]

The Woriax Family history reads, Sarah Elizabeth Hardin (1853-1955) married Enoch Manuel (1846-1927), 28 Dec 1909. Sarah parents were: Amos "Si" Hardin (Harding) and Lanie Jackson (white) alias Cassie Lockamy, Irish descent.

Henry Frank Hardin's (27 Aug 1877-16 Jun 1949) parents were: Frederick Hardin and Mary Graham. Walden Hardin (11 Sep 1879-12 Oct 1965) married Fannie Hagen (1889-1980). Their daughter, Stella Jane Hardin Locklear Oxendine (1 May 1912-6 Apr 2012) married George Locklear.

In the 1880 US Census, dwelling #134, family #135, lived Esquire Bell (24), his wife, Caroline (23). Esquire was listed as a farmer. Their children: Sohiah (F, 5 years) and John A. (M, 7 years).

James Ernest Bell (15 Nov 1886-17 Dec 1947) was a merchant.

William and Hellen [Bell] Santee's children: Lucy Ann, Mary Jane, William J, Farme, and H.B. Also, Lonza Santee (1855), his wife (1863), and children: Jane and William (Feb 1880).

Writer discovered Robert Bell (1790-4 Feb 1866) living in Charleston, SC. In 1850, he moved to Marion, GA. He was Head of Household of the following persons: Ann Bell (age 30); Hista [Esther] Bell (age 25); Mary Lowery (abt. 1826, age 24); Elizabeth Bell (age 22) Margret Bell (age 21); Samuel Bell (abt. 1830); and, Charlotte Bell (age 18).

Bell, Robert, Pvt., served in the Civil War through the AL Calvary. He was held as a prisoner of war (POW) at Andersonville. He died in Andersonville with complications from Dysentery, 3 Aug 1864. Robert married Sarah, 1833. The family lived in Covington, Rose Hill, AL. His son, Samuel Bell, also served in the Civil War through AL.

Apparently, this Robert Bell was a descend of the elder Pvt. Samuel Bell, or a member of additional Samuel Bells who served in the Revolutionary War.

---

[31] Ibid., pp. 550 &-556.

Researching the 31 May 1880, Robeson County Mortality List, writer discovered "Silvy" Hammond, died in Sep, (age 64). This was Sylvania "Silva" Roberts (1815-Sep 1879), the wife of Ollen Hammonds, alias Willis Hammonds (1774-1832), the son of Horatio Hammonds (1744-1810) and Patience Brayboy, whose parents were: John [David] and Lydia Brayboy. Willis Hammonds married Martha A. West (1775-Oct 1850), 1793.

Ollen and Silva Roberts Hammonds' children: George Washington Hammonds (1820-10 Jul 1923); Anderson Hammonds (1840) married Nancy Hunt; Joanna Hammonds (1841-7 Aug 1928) married Jonathan "John" Hunt (1842-1896); and, William Hammond (1832-19 Sep 1925) was buried in the Roberts Graveyard, Lumberton, NC. Johanna and Jonathan "Little John" Hunt's son was Sweeten Hunt (10 Oct 1864-3 Apr 1914).

Sweeten Hunt married Strawdie Oxendine, 4 Apr 1885. Sweeten Hunt married Victoria Johnson (1878-14 Dec 1945), 10 Jan 1897.

George Washington Hammonds married Caroline Smith Carter (15 Mar 1839-28 Nov 1929). She was buried in the SA Hammonds Cemetery, Lumberton, NC. Their son, Rev. Stephen A. Hammonds married Sarah Margaret Bell. Their daughter, Lela Jane married John J. Brooks, the son of Alexander "Sandy" Brooks and Effie Jane Hunt, a member of the Lewis Hunt family.

According to George Washington Hammonds' NC Death Certificate, his father is listed as Ollin [Ollen] Hammonds and his mother as Perella Porter Lawsen (1817; grave marker 15 Jul 1798-1 Jan 1890).

Pvt. George Washington Hammonds (d. 1945), who served in the Confederate War in Company E, 2nd NC Regiment, was buried in the Family [Hammons] Cemetery, Saddletree, Lumberton, NC, signed by S.A. Hammonds.[32]

Additional persons listed on the 1880 Mortality list were: BS Barnes, died Oct, possible, a relative to John A. Barnes. Mary Holmes, died Jan, (age 70, abt. 1810). Lucy Thompson died Nov 1879, (age 70, abt. 1809). J.E. Smith was born in SC and died Sep 1879, (abt. 1824, age 55).

---

[32] Cummings-Woriax, *American Indian Patriots*, p. 110.

No doubt, Mary Holmes (1810-Nov 1879) was the daughter of Anna Hammonds, formerly of Cumberland County. Anna married Primus Jacobs, 4 Mar 1826, Cumberland County.

Jacobs, Primus (abt. 1745-23 Jul 1834), Pvt., S41688, served in the NC Continental Line through New Hanover County, NC. On 1 Nov 1819, Primus Jacobs, age 60, applied for his war pension. He married Anna Hammonds, 4 Mar 1826. In 1820, he was Head of (5) Household Members. One infant son, Primus Jacobs (Nov 1819-24 May 1820).

Primus Jacobs was formerly married to Rebecca (NKA). Rebecca, his widow, who was living in NH, rejected claim.

Lucy Thompson (1824-1879) married Hugh Thompson (31 Jan 1803-5 Apr 1871), 26 Jun 1826. Hugh was buried in the historical Asbury Methodist Church, Rhynam, NC. The church sits beside Highway NC 130 East, between Rowland and Fairmont, NC. The early Scots who entered Robeson County, gave churches and communities the names of their former homes in England. For example, Rhynam is such a namesake.

Younger Hardy Holmes Bell (3 Feb 1856-30 Apr 1921) married Narcissus "Sis" or "Rsil" Hammons (10 Aug 1861-19 Nov 1933), 21 Mar 1878. Narcissus' parents were: George Washington Hammonds (abt. 1820-10 Jul 1923) and Caroline Carter (15 Mar 1839-28 Nov 1929).

One Narcissus "Sis" or "Rsil" was also listed as a Monroe, the granddaughter of Mariah Locklear, the wife of Needham Locklear. Her maternal grandfather was Jerry Prevatt who married Rosa Ann [Roxan "Ciss"] Monroe (1841-1915). Mariah's father was Jerry Prevatt or Prevatte.

Sis Monroe's children were: Baxley; John; Eddie; Bertha; Gabbie; and, Roxanna (1 Jan 1870-6 Dec 1946) married James A. Locklear (d. 1918). Gabbie Monroe's (1883-1959) grave marker reads Gabby Monroe Carter. He was buried in the Christian Cemetery, Lumberton, NC.

Bertha L. Monroe (15 May 1878-22 Nov 1959) married John Blanks, 21 Feb 1894. John's parents were: Narcissus Bell (10 Aug 1861-19 Nov 1933) and Hardy Holmes Bell. John and Bertha's son, John Clarence Blanks (15 Aug 1898-2 Jan 1950) married Bessie Locklear, 30 Oct 1918.

Hardy Holmes and Narcissus Bell's daughter was Martha Jane Bell (1 Dec 1882-16 May 1924).

In the 1880 US Census, writer discovered Sarah Parker Bell (abt. 1796, age 84) listed as a widow, Howellsville, Robeson County, dwelling #135, family #136, line #3.

Writer discovered Sally Parker (1800) was listed as a widow. She was born in New Hampshire, USA. Sally Parker died, Jan 1889.

Also, in the 1880 US Census, dwelling #133, family #134, lived Semone [Seymour] Bell (age 43), and wife, Elizer (age 30). Seymour was listed as a farmer. In dwelling #324, family #324, lived Catherine Gilbert and her children and the following persons: Laina [Lavina] Gilbert (abt. 1796, age 84), and Lucy Ivey (abt. 1807, age 73) listed as a Pauper.

Writer has unanswered questions concerning Thomas Hagans (1809) who was living in SC and his relationship to Fannie Hagan. Thomas Hagans was the grandfather of Thomas Ivey who married Mollie Kinlaw. Also, Thomas Ivey (NC) was a family member to Lucy Ivey. She was listed in the Catherine Gilbert family, Robeson County, NC.

Hagan, Thomas (1809), served in the Civil War through SC.

Mary E. Blanks married John Hardin (1848-11 Jan 1936), the son of Dolphus and Harriett Hardin.

Blanks, Sr., John Blanks (1750-?), Pvt., served through the VA 6th Regiment in the Revolutionary War. John received a Land Grant in 1773, Bladen County, NC.

Another, John Blanks (d. 1798), was listed as a Mulatto, whose son was Alfred Blanks. John Blanks lived in Hanover and Bladen Counties NC and Richland County, SC.

Blanks, John (1820-?), Pvt., served in the Civil War through Company A, North Carolina 31st Infantry Regiment. He married Aley Ivey (1817), 12 Jan 1842.

John and Aley Ivey Blank's children were: James W., John A., and Mary E.

John Blanks (1842) and Rosella Blanks' son, Alfred Blanks (23 Mar 1879-12 May 1934), lived in Council, NC.

Blanks, James W. (12 Apr 1847-27 Jan 1912), Pvt., served in the Civil War through the North Carolina Company F, 51st Infantry Regiment, Robeson County. James W. was wounded to his shoulder in the battle at Ft. Drewry's Bluff. James was then transferred to a hospital in Richmond, VA. Ft. Drewry's Bluff is also known as Fort Darling.

James married Sarah C. Bell, a descend of Revolutionary War soldier, Samuel Bell. Rev. James Blanks served as a clergyperson in the early Burnt Swamp Indian Association, Robeson County, NC. He was buried in the Ten Mile Center Baptist Church Cemetery, Lumberton, NC.

John Clarence Blanks (15 Aug 1898-2 Jan 1950) married Bessie Locklear. Bessie Blanks was the pianist at Bear Swamp Baptist Church. In the late 1950's she married James Wadis Wilkins (1898-1968) following the death of his wife, Rosie Oxendine. Ms. Rosie (1908-1954) was one of the former pianists at Bear Swamp Baptist Church.

First Lt. Hardy Holmes Family

Holmes, Hardy, First Lt., entered the Revolutionary War in 1782. Hardy Holmes was born 13 Jun 1749, England. His father was John Holmes, a Citizen and Cooper of London. He was employed as an apprentice to Thomas Brown. Hardy worked for seven years to learn the art under Brown. Hardy was paid Forty-five pounds. He was then qualified to teach and instruct others in fine fame art.[33] [See Admission Papers Image II, p. 91.]

Hardy's mother was, Mesta Thomas Brown, perhaps, the daughter of Hardy's instructor Thomas Brown.

According to Lt. Hardy Holmes' war Pension, a Bounty-Land-Warrant application file, May 31, 1798, no papers were filed. He entered the Revolutionary War in 1782 and was discharged Feb 1783. In 1790, Hardy (abt. 1750), lived in and died, 14 Jul 1828, Sampson County, NC. Hardy was enumerated 7 August 1820, Sampson County, NC.

Another Hardy Holmes, or the same, Capt. Hardy Holmes (abt. 1740), served in the Continental Army. Writer discovered another Hardy Holmes who died, 11 Sep 1819.

The following marriage information was abstracted from the Moore Grave Marker, Turkey, NC. Lt. Hardy Holmes married Fereba Moore (17

---

[33] London, England Freedom of the City Admission Papers 1681-1930. (data base on line). ancestry.com

Mar 1764), the daughter of James Moore (14 Nov 1729) and Ann Thomson (29 Aug 1739). [See Moore Grave Marker, Image IV, p. 92.]

James' parents were: Joseph and Ann Hodges Moore, Edgecombe County, NC. In 1790, Hardy Holmes was found listed in the Duplin County census as Head of (2) Household Members. In the 1800 Sampson County census, Hardy Holmes was Head of (2) Household Members and (16) Slaves.

Hardy Holmes lived in Robeson County in 1830 near John L. Holmes, Hardy Bell, Ainy Holmes, and Capt. Jacob Blount. In 1756, John Holmes was living in Bladen County.

1st Lt. Hardy Holmes was buried in the Thompson-Moore Family Cemetery, Turkey, Sampson County, NC. His grave marker is faded due to being weather worn. Hardy Holmes' NC Will and Probate Record, p. 407, Sampson County Deeds Office. [See Hardy Holmes Grave Marker photo Image III, p. 91.]

Ann Richard Holmes (1763-Aug 1849, age 86). Ann's NC Will and Probate Deed, p. 409, was filed at the Sampson County Deed office. No record was discovered to indicate if Ann Holmes was Hardy's wife. Further research is required.

In 1820, Ann Richard Holmes was enumerated 7 Aug 1820 as Head of (4) Household Member and (23) Slaves.

Hardy Holmes was listed in the early Tax List, 1784. Archibald Holmes was listed in the 1767 early Tax List.

Also, the following two women were associated with Hardy Holmes and his son, Hardy Lucian Holmes. Mary N. Holmes [the daughter of Gabriel and Mildred L. Holmes] and Margaret Holmes.

Holmes, Gabriel (21 Dec 1786-23 Sep 1848), Pvt., lived in Sampson County as earlier as 1788. He was issued a Land Grant for 200 acres of land near Little Cohera [Coharie] River. In 1799, another 600 acres of land was granted. Gabriel Holmes died 23 Sep 1848, Cumberland County. He married Mildred L. Molson [Mabson], (1791-22 Aug 1835), Sampson County, then moved to live in Wilmington, NC.

Gabriel Holmes from Sampson County, then Wilmington, became Governor of NC. Apparently, he was a son or brother to Hardy Holmes. Writer discovered Gabriel Holmes' name listed on NC Marriages licenses.

Hardy's son, Hardy Lucian Holmes (1795-1869), Sampson County, attended the University of Chapel Hill. Lucian graduated with an A.B. degree in 1817. Lucian set up his law practice in Wilmington, NC. A son, Lucian Holmes (1826) became an Episcopal Clergyperson.[34]

The following persons were among those listed with Hardy Holmes: Lewis Holmes, Owen Holmes, Gabriel Holmes, Benjamin Bell, Jesse Bell, all living in Sampson County.

First Sgt. Gabriel Holmes married Lucy Drew, 6 Nov 1824, Halifax, NC. The surname Drew is an Indian surname, Halifax, NC.

One Gabriel Holmes served in the Civil War. He entered the war through Sampson County, 16 Apr 1862.

Jesse Bell was listed in the Sampson County 1790 census as a Slave. A brother, Robert Bell (29 Feb 1772) received 100 acres of land on Stag Branch, 9 Apr 1769.

Bell, Jesse (1830-2 Mar 1861), Pvt., served in the Civil War through the 1st Mille's Battery Cavalry; 1st Montgomery Battery Cavalry; and in the 1st Choctaw Battle, Pontotoc, Mississippi (MS).

Writer discovered Sarah Holmes (1763) and her family living in New Hanover near Colvins Creek, NC.

According to the Robeson County 1880 Mortality list, Mary Holmes, died Jan, (age 70). Mary Holmes (1809-Nov 1879) was the daughter of Anna Hammonds, formerly of Cumberland County, NC.[35]

Holmes, John (1756) Bladen County, entered the Revolutionary War in summer of 1777. He served for 4 years in the NC Continental Line, through Capt. Mills Co. He reenlisted on 18 Dec 1781 and served for 12 months; later

---

[34] The U.S. School Catalogs, 1765-1935 for Hardy Holmes, p. 64 (1820), NC Un of NC, 1795. ancestry.com.
[35] The Robeson County 1880 Morality, Ancestry.com

becoming a Justice of Peace, Brunswick County. His 2nd pension application was filed, 7 Feb 1852. John was issued a Land Grant 15 Dec 1778, Bk 32, P. 10, Duplin County, NC.

In the 1850 Duplin County census John Holmes was (age 73); Louis (age 3) was blind; Ann M (age 37); Stephen (age 33), worked as a Cooper; Nancy (age 22); and, Louisa (age 17). All were listed as Mulattoes living in Duplin County, NC. John Holmes Last Will and Testament was dated 1853, Duplin, NC.

Duplin County John Holmes is often confused with Pvt. John Holmes, Brunswick County, NC. [See Pvt. John Holmes Revolutionary War deposition on p. 28.] He did not receive any county land of the US, dated 30 Apr 1829.

John married Swanee [Florence Swan] McLean (May 1881-24 Jul 1914), the daughter of Henrietta Brigman. John Holmes and Swanee daughters were: Emma Laura, Ethel, and Dovie Holmes (1898), who married Tommie Allen (1 Mar 1895-5 Oct 1963), the son of Sandy Allen and Josephine Holmes, whose parents were: Macon Holmes and Margaret Young.

Dovie and John's son was Howard L. [Luke] Holmes. Dovie was buried in the Richmond County Memorial Park, Rockingham, NC.

Howard Allen served in the US Army, WWII. His uncle, Howard L. Holmes signed his Draft Card. Howard's parents were: Howard Luke Allen and Georgia Mae Holmes. Georgia Allen Holmes Troxler (28 Jun 1903-1973) was buried in the Hillside Cemetery, Laurinburg, NC.[36]

---

[36] Cummings-Woriax, *American Indian Patriots*, p. 209.

Pvt. Moses Carter

Carter, Moses, Pvt., S41470, Cumberland County, NC, served in the 1st Regiment NC Line, Continental, 1 Aug 1782 for 18 months through Sampson County in the Revolutionary War. Moses took a leave of absence, 19 Jul 1782. He married Ann Walker, 17 Jun 1779, New Hanover. In 1780, he lived in Anson County, NC. Moses signed his name with an "M." In 1790, he was Head of (9) Household members. In 1805, he was issued a Land Grant. An application was made for his war pension, 24 Oct 1820, at (83) years-of-age.

A war pension was issued 24 Oct 1820, for one Colored Moses Carter, 4 Jan 1821. In 1821, Moses was married to Tobiha White, Craven, NC. Moses was previously married to Matilda Hammon, Beaufort, NC, the daughter of Virginia Hammond (1805).

Hardy L. [Lucian] Holmes, Sampson County, NC, served as the lawyer for Pvt. Moses Carter. His war pension payment, 1 Qtr. 1822, Fayetteville, NC. Lawyer Holmes, was overseer for Moses Carter property, 26 Oct 1820. Moses Carter died 18 Mar 1818.

Bell, Holmes, and Carter Families

In her critical research, writer discovered who she believed to be a brother or near relative to Samuel Bell living in Halifax, NC. His name was Arthur Bell (d. 10 Jun 1775). Arthur Bell was married to Elizabeth. According to the Edgecombe Court NC Deeds, Elizabeth Bell's dower deeded, 20 Jan 1774 from Arthur Bell was relinquished by Nathan Boddie and Matthew Drake, in the Oct Court 1774.

In Arthur Bell's Last Will and Testament, he provided the names of his children: Joshua, Shadrack, Elisha, Lucy, Mary, Sarah, and Absilla, a daughter-in-law. Absilla married Benjamin Bell. An additional family member was John Drew and Arthur's horse, Dolphin. It is possible that John Drew could be a relative to Lucy Drew, 6 Nov 1824, Halifax, NC. Drew families did enter and live in Robeson County, NC. More research is required.

Another Arthur Bell (1751), served in the Revolutionary War. His military pension commenced, 4 Mar 1831.

Bell, Benjamin, Corpl., lived in Pasquotank County. He served in the Revolutionary War through the North Carolina 2nd Regiment Infantry, 1778. His father was Arthur Bell (d. 10 Jun 1775), Halifax, NC. His wife was Elizabeth. Their son was Marmaduke N. Bell. Benjamin married Rebeckah [Rebecca] Johnson, 8 Feb 1815.

According to Arthur Bell's Last Will and Testament, Benjamin's wife was Absilla Bell.

Hardy Holmes Bell's daughter, Harriet Bell (1827-10 Nov 1892) married Dolphin Hardin (1818), 10 Jan 1844. Their son, Daniel Holmes married Alle Revels, 25 Feb 1868, whose parents were: Elijah Revels (1813) and Susan "Sookie" Carter (26 Mar 1823-11 Jun 1895), 30 Dec 1843.

Elijah and Susan's son, William "Billy" Revels (1857-1937) married Maggie Locklear. Susan was buried in the Revels-Hammonds Cemetery, Saddletree Community, Lumberton, NC. Elijah's parents were: Edmund Revils (1725), Nash County, and Sabre (NKA), Forsyth County, NC.

Alle and Daniel's daughter, Mollie Holmes (1875-23 Mar 1950) married Riley Angus Chavis (20 Jun 1860-20 Jun 1925). Mollie and Riley Angus' children were: Tracy, Garfield, and two infants who died at birth.[37]

Daniel B. Holmes married Stella Mercer. They lived at Sea Green, NC. His parents were: Daniel and Jane Holmes.

Revels, Elijah (1725-1807; alt. date 1750-Nov 1807), Pvt., died in Nash County, NC. He served in the Revolutionary War through Sampson County, NC. His parents were: Edmound Revels (1725), Nash County, NC and Sabra [NKA], Forsyth County, NC. He married Dolly [Burden], (1747-1811). In the 1790 census, Edmound was living in Wayne County, NC.

For his service to his country, Elijah was awarded six hundred and forty acres (640) of land in NC, 30 Sep 1785. He wrote his Last Will and Testament, 1807, with instructions as to whom and what items each was to receive.[38]

Elijah and Dollie's daughter, Beda [Betsy], (1780-1855) married Jesse Manuell, Sampson County, NC. They later migrated to Greene County, TN. Elijah Revels son, Nathaniel Revels married Elizabeth Lowrie. Their son, Frederick "Fredric" (1827-1 Oct 1902) married Jane "Jeannie" Goins (1837-abt. 1890). His second marriage was to Frances Hardin.

Elijah Revels (1813) and Susan "Sookie" Carter's daughter, Alle Revels married Daniel Holmes, 25 Feb 1868. Daniel's parents were: Harriet Bell

---

[37] Cummings-Woriax, *Creation*, pp. 542 & 550.
[38] Ibid., p. 561.

(1827-10 Nov 1892) and Dolphin Bell (1818), 10 Jan 1844. Harriet was the daughter of Hardy Holmes Bell.

Narcesus Brigman married William Paul. Their daughter, Della (1862-13 Nov 1922), lived in Red Bluff, SC. Della married [NKA] Driggers [former Rodrigus, Portuguese].

Another daughter, Mary Ann Paul Carter alias Nancy Ann Paul (17 Mar 1855-20 Jul 1917) married Richard R. Chavis. No doubt, Richard R. [Chavis] Carter's (1832-10 Mar 1915) mother was Rachel Chavis (1803/1811-1833) prior to her marriage to James Carter (1794/1810-1850), 17 Mar 1830.

Rachel and James Carter's children were: Richard R. Carter and Huldah Carter (14 Apr 1840-21 Oct 1922). Richard was born in Montgomery County, NC.

Huldah married Charles Moore. She later married Sherrod Hunt, 7 Nov 1859, Robeson County, NC.

Rachel Carter (1855) married Levi Chavis (1849). Rachel's parents were: Richard and Helen Carter, 29 Aug 1849. Rachel married John F. Oxendine, whose parents were: Charles W. and Nancy J. Clarke Oxendine. Levi Chavis married Deliah Goins, 2 Oct 1816.

A younger Rachel Carter (1869-17 May 1934) married Furney Sanderson.

Rachel Carter Chavers/Chavis married Thomas Sampson, 6 Jun 1827, Robeson County, NC. Thomas Sampson's parents were: Joseph Sampson (1812) and Fannie.[39]

Sampson, Thomas (1802- abt. 1885), served in the B 7 YS Infantry in the Civil War. He married Rachel Carter [Chavers], (1830-10 Mar 1915), 6 Jun 1827, Robeson County, NC. Rachel's parents were: Richard and Helen Carter. Richard married Mary Ann Paul (12 Mar 1855-20 Jul 1917). Apparently, according to his war pension information, Thomas became an invalid 30 Apr 1885 and died before 1899. He was buried in the Carter-Chavis Cemetery, Pembroke, NC. Rachel Sampson's first war pension began 15 Jun 1899, Maryland.

---

[39] Ibid, pp. 58 & 220.

In the Robeson County 1820 census Thomas Sampson was Head of (4) Free Whites and (1) Slave. His enumeration date was 7 Aug 1820.

Thomas Sampson married Elvie Hammons. Their son, Henry H. [Hammonds] Sampson (23 Dec 1804-3 Apr 1874) married Nancy Carter (20 Dec 1802-18 Nov 1897), 29 Sep 1828, Cumberland County, NC. Their daughter was Henrietta (d. 1914). Henry H. Hammonds, Sr., was buried in the Deep Branch Baptist Church Cemetery, Lumberton, NC. And younger Henry H. Sampson (29 Apr 1861-24 Sep 1927) was buried in the Deep Branch Baptist Church Cemetery.

However, Henry Hammonds' father was Pvt. James Hammonds who fought with the Mounted Volunteers in the Mexican War.

According to writer's family resource, an Ida Brooks Locklear Strong married a Chavis. Their daughter was Minnie Chavis. Ida's parents were: Augustus Angus Chavis and Hosanna. Hosanna's daughter, Ida Brook Chavis married Boss Strong, a brother to Rhoda Strong. Ida was living with Henry and Nancy Carter Sampson in 1870. Ida Chavis later married Frank Cummings, the son of Elisha Cummings and Mary Locklear, SC, the daughter of Joseph "Chief Joe" and Amurie [Susan America] Evans.

Elisha Cummings (1834-23 Oct 1908, NC), served as a SC Confederate Soldier through 1 (Butler's) SC Infantry 1st Regiment, 1st Regulars. He was held as a prisoner of war (POW) in GA. His parents were: Enoch Cummins, Sr., and Winnie Tetter. Enoch Cummins was this writer's paternal (5x) great-grandfather.

Caroline Carter (1839-1930) married George Washington Hammonds. Caroline and George's son, Stephen Andrew "SA" Hammonds (abt. 1877-1951) married Florence Revels (abt. 1873-). SA and Florence's children were: Docia Hammonds (1900-1972) and Lela Jane Hammonds who married John J. Brooks. John' parents were: Alexander "Sandy" Brooks and Effie Jane Hunt. Sandy and Effie were this writer's maternal (3x) great-grandparents.

Sandy was the maternal grandson of both Revolutionary War soldiers, John Brooks and William Lowrie [Loughery]. Lela's second husband was Rev. Clarence Eden Locklear. His parents were: Archie Locklear and Mary Frances Locklear of the Prospect Community, Maxton, NC. In 1919, Rev. Clarence Eden Locklear was ordained at the Mt. Airy Baptist Church, Pembroke, NC.

According to the Brooks Family records, Lela Jane Hammonds' parents were: Rev. S.A. Hammonds (30 Jun 1874-2 Apr 1951) and Sarah Margaret Bell (1 Dec 1885-10 Dec 1967). Rev. Hammonds was a member of the early George Washington and Carolina [Caroline] Hammons Family.

Lillie Mae Smith (1902-1993) was the daughter of Hugh Smith (12 Mar 1866-2 Jun 1947) and Ida Pone (17 Nov 1871-5 Oct 1980). Ida's father was Ezekiel "Zeke" Pone (6 Oct 1849-5 Jul 1925), the son of Alexander "Alex" Pone who served in the Revolutionary War. Hugh and Ida were buried in the Bethel Hill Church Cemetery.

Ezekiel married Henrietta "Etta" Thompson (15 Sep 1849-19 Jun 1918), whose father was B.S. Thompson. Their son, Arthur Pone, was murdered, 23 Apr 1910, by Tom Brayboy. Arthur Pone was buried in the Cummings Family Cemetery, Union Chapel Road, Pembroke, NC. Ezekiel married Lula Carter (1883-31 Dec 1952), the daughter of Alonzo "Lonzy" Carter (19 Sep 1876-13 Oct 1960).

Henrietta "Etta's" brother, Civil D. Thompson Callahan (4 Dec 1856-4 Jul 1937) was buried in the Old Field Cemetery, Bladen County. His father was Benjamin [Thompson] who married Mary J., prior to her marriage to C. C. Callahan.[40]

Charlie Neil Smith's (23 Apr 1885-23 Aug 1959) parents were: Daniel C. Smith and Katie Knight. Charlie Neil married Mardella Wilkins (1 Jul 1893; alt. date Aug 1919-26 Jan 1968), whose parents were: Sion Wilkins and Sarah Ann Revels [Wellington Wilkins and Bessie Jacobs]. Charlie Neil and Mardella were buried in the Cummings Family Cemetery, Pembroke, NC.

---

[40] Cummings-Woriax, *Creation*, p. 424.

The Peter Port Family

In 1790, Peter Port (1750), Corpl., served in the Revolutionary War. In 1790, he and his wife, Sarah, lived in Bladen County. Their daughter, Sarah Jane Port married J. T. Lowrimore. In 1819, Peter and his family lived in Marion County, SC. In 1820, they lived in Georgetown, SC. And, in 1840, the Port's lived in Fayetteville, NC.

In 1820, Peter Port married June Carter, 9 May 1820, Cumberland County, NC. Peter Port was enumerated 7 August 1820, SC. Following David Carter's death in 1842, Peter Port provided care to David's children and was the executor of Carter's property, Cumberland County, NC.

A younger Peter Port (1832), Corpl., served as a Confederate War soldier in Ward's Company, South Carolina (Waccamaw) Light Artillery, as a Gunner. Peter Port was enumerated 12 Jun 1880. He married Sarah Parker (1832).

Peter and Sarah's son, Benjamin Franklin Port (22 Aug 1853-24 Apr 1919), Horry County, SC, married Mary Ann Strickland, 4 Apr 1874, Waccamaw, NC. At his death, Benjamin was married to Rebecca Woodward. Benjamin was employed as a Ferryman. In the 1850 census, Sarah Parker Port and Cornelius Port (1810) were living in Cumberland County, NC.

William Fort

Researching the Bell Family and additional Revolutionary War soldiers in the Saddletree and the Ten Mile Communities, this writer discovered Capt. John E. Willis (NC, prior 1759-22 Apr 1802, LA). He fought in the NC Continental Line as a Whig soldier and in the Revolutionary War. Willis is recognized as the "father of Lumberton."

John married Asenath Barnes (NC, 1761/1763-1807, MS). Asenath's parents were: Abraham "Abram" Barnes and Martha [Matilda] Fort (VA, 1730/1745-24 Jan 1794, NC), 1750. Abraham was a Revolutionary War soldier and Martha's parents were: George Fort and Mary Catherine Fort.

Was William Fort a former Revolutionary War soldier? Writer failed to discover William Fort listed as a soldier. Fort was issued a Land Grant, 1748, Bladen County. Samuel Bell's Family history suggest and the North Carolina State Census list the following persons living in early Halifax County, NC - Elias Fort, Sugans Fort, John Fort, and Allen Fort.

On 8 Oct 1775, Elias Fort, Craven County, SC, sold his portion of land to Jacob Fort, Edgecombe County who paid 30 pounds for 453 acres in the St. Mary Parich [Parish], joining George Fort and others. Witness Joseph Fort and others, Jan court 1775.

In Bladen County, Elias [Elijah] Fort was issued a Land Grant at Panthers Branch in 1756. Joseph Fort was issued two Land Grant at Ten Mile, 17 Mar

1756 and Saddletree, 26 Nov 1757. Could William Fort be a member of the George Fort's family?

In 1736, Robert Lowry received a NC land grant for six hundred and forty acres (640) of land, Bladen County near the Lumber River. Also, Robert Lowry, Jr., received a NC land grant for six hundred and forty acres (640) in 1736. In 1748, Henry [O'Berry] Berry [Jr.] and James Lowrie (d. 1752) purchased 100 acres of land from William Fort [from Surry County] who received the Land Grant from King George, II.[41]

On 2 Feb 1754, Henry O'Berry purchased 500 acres at Drowning Creek. The land was formerly owned by William Hull.

In the 1790 census, Abraham Barnes was Head of (1) and (8) Slaves. Abraham and Martha were the parents of (13) children. Additional children: Josiah Fort, Elias, and Mary. Martha was buried in Robeson County.

Abraham's children were listed in his Last Will and Testament, 1794, Vol 1-2, 1787-1869. Josiah, Elias, Asenath, Bridgers, and Mary. Josiah was buried in the Barnes Cemetery, Port Gibson, MS. Several daughters: Susan, Harriett, and Asenath (NC, 1761-1806) died in Natchez, MS. Members of the Fort family were living in Mississippi around 1780.

---

[41] Cummings-Woriax, *Creation*, pp. 136 & 161.

Direct Descendant of Pvt. Samuel Bell, Sgt. (Retired) William Ronald "Pete" Bell

Samuel Bell, Revolutionary War Soldier direct descendants.

Son - Hardy H. Bell (abt. 1766/1786-28 Apr 1866) and Sarah "Sallie" Parker married 1820, Cumberland County, NC.

Grandson - Hardy H. Bell (3 Feb 1856-30 Apr 1921) married Narcissus "Sis" Hammons (10 Aug 1861-19 Nov 1933), 21 Mar 1878. Her parents were: George Washington Hammons (abt. 1820-10 Jul 1923) and Caroline Carter (15 Mar 1839-28 Nov 1929, age 104).

Great-grandson - Wiley Daniel "Willie" Bell (31 Aug 1831-9 Aug 1909). Apparently, the following Wiley or Willie Bell (Mar 1887) was the son of Wiley Daniel Bell (Mar 1887). According to his, Wiley or Willie Bell's WWI Draft Card, his exception read: he had been wounded.

In 1910, Willie Bell lived in Bulloch, GA. Others listed in the census were: Andrew "Ander" Bell (Head), Maggie Locklear Bell (spouse), Benj. F. Bell, Hattie W. Bell, and Romas D. Bell. Willie was listed as a brother to Andrew (1866). Andrew became known as Rev. William A. Bell (22 May 1889-7 Jan 1970). William A. Bell and Maggie Locklear Bell (10 Nov 1889-27 Apr 1950). She was buried in the Antioch Baptist Church Cemetery, Lumberton, NC.

Andrew "Ander" Bell married Maggie Locklear (8 Oct 1895-10 May 1953), whose parents were: James Locklear (1875-5 Sep 1896) and Martha "Lady" Locklear (1876-1914), whose parents were: Daniel Locklear (8 Jun 1838-12 Jan 1902) and Zenith "Edith" Locklear (1842-27 Mar 1902), 10 Jan 1862.

James Locklear's parents were: Calvin Locklear (1829) and Mary Locklear (abt. 1835-1900), the daughter of Malinda Locklear and (NKA) Chavis. Malinda later married Oliver Revels.

Great-great-grandson – Hardy Bell (3 Feb 1856-30 Apr 1921).

Great-great-great-grandson - Furman Belford Bell (5 Jan 1905-22 Aug 1981).

Great-great-great-great- grandson: William Ronald "Pete" Bell, served in the US Marine Corps in the Vietnam War.

Furman Bell's Siblings:

1. Leaner Bell Burnett (1883-11 Jun 1914).
2. William A. [Ander] Bell (GA, 22 May 1889-7 Jan 1970).
3. George W. Bell (20 Apr 1889-4 May 1976), Pvt.
4. Governor C. Bell (22 Sep 1895-11 Mar 1946), US Army, WWI.
5. Stephen Frank Bell (14 Sep 1896-2 Dec 1961), PFC., US Army, WWI.
6. James Edmond Bell (15 Jun 1899-18 Dec 1988), US Army, WWI.
7. Hattie Bell Canady (3 Sep 1901-5 Oct 2000).

Furman Belford Bell married Maggie J. Lockley [Locklear], (30 Dec 1909-20 Mar 2008), 9 May 1927 at the Sheriff's office in Dunn, Harnett County, NC. Maggie's parents were: "Jus L. Locklear," James L. Locklier (SC, 26 Oct 1876-7 Oct 1970, NC) and Charlotte Groves (28 Oct 1884-7 Jun 1973), the daughter of James Groves and Azella Maynor, 28 Sep 1902, Harnett County, NC. Charlotte worked in the horse stables in the city of Lumberton.

James and Charlotte's children: John Leach Locklear, served in the US Army, WWII; Edward Locklear; and, additional children.

Furman and Maggie Locklear Bell's children:

1. Helen Narcissus "Arciss" Bell (9 Jan 1927-10 Oct 2010).
2. Ruby Pearl Bell Chavis (16 Jan 1929-18 Oct 2008).
3. James Furman "Buddy" Bell (19 Aug 1931-24 Dec 2014), US Army, Korea War.
4. Belford Lee Bell (9 Nov 1933-14 Mar 1952).
5. Gladys "Tony" Von Fect.
6. Kathryn Robinson.
7. Glennis Bell Hunt.
8. Sgt., William Ronald "Pete" Bell (2 Aug 1944), served in the US Marine Corps in the Vietnam War. He married Susan Rebecca Thompson, St. Pauls, NC.

Hardy Holmes Bell's parents were: Hardy H. Bell (abt. 1766-28 Apr 1866) and Sarah "Sallie" Parker (1800-1880).

Furman Belford's parents were: Willie Bell and Maggie Groves Locklear. Willie's parents were Hardy Holmes Bell (3 Feb 1856-30 Apr 1921) and Narcissus "Sis" or "Rsil" Hammons (10 Aug 1861-19 Nov 1933) married 21 Mar 1878.

William Ronald "Pete" Bell (2 Aug 1944), Sgt., served in the US Marines Corps, 1st Marine Division, in the Vietnam War. And, retired from the NC Army Reserves. His parents were: Furman Belford Bell (5 Jan 1905-22 Aug 1981) and Maggie Lockley [Locklear], 9 May 1927, Harnett County, NC.

Pvt. William Ronald "Pete" Bell married Susan Rebecca Thompson.

William "Pete" is a direct descend of Pvt. Samuel Bell, Revolutionary War Patriot, born in Halifax County, VA (1749). Samuel entered the war through Sampson County, NC. He served in the Col. Lytle's NC Regiment. Pvt. Samuel Bell lived in Sampson County, Robeson County, Cumberland County, and Duplin County, NC. His enumeration date 7 August 1820.

Sgt. William Ronald "Pete" Bell is a member of the NC Sons of the American Revolution (NCSAR), le Marquis de Lafayette. He entered the US

Marine Corps, 18 Apr 1969; discharged 1970; entered the NC National Army Reserves, 1973; discharged 1992.

Sgt. William R. Bell was awarded the following Medals and/or Ribbons for his service in the Vietnam War and the NC Army National Guard:

The National Defense Medal x2; the Army Service Medal x1; the Combat Action Ribbon; the Meritorious Unit Commendation; the Army Reserve Components Achievement Medal/Ribbons x4; the Humanitarian Service Medal; the Vietnam Civil Action Medal; the Vietnam Service Medal; the NC Meritorious Unit Commendation Medal; the Republic of Vietnam Campaign Medal; the Republic of Vietnam Gallantry Cross Unit Citation with PALM; the Army Reserve Components Overseas Training Ribbon; and the Armed Forces Reserve Medal.

The Samuel Bell descends then and today continue to live on the Saddle Tree Swamp, some ten or twelve miles from Lumberton on the Old Stage Road from Lumberton to Fayetteville. One member of the family in the mid to late 1800's was Hardy Bell. According to the census he was living in Robeson County around 1840. Hardy began a goods store on what is known as the banks of the Lumber River. He became one of, if not the most successful merchant in Lumberton until his death. Writer discovered various business transaction between he and others in the Robeson County Deed Book.

Grady Locklear's resource focuses on Hardy Bell's land and its value. Whereas, author, Mary C. Norment in her book makes reference to the merchandise business which she describes "as a burlesque."[42]

Sgt. Bell and his family continue to live in the Saddletree Community on property which his ancestor Hardy Holmes Bell and his (5x) great-grandfather, Samuel Bell received through Bladen County Land Grants following the Revolutionary War.

---

[42] Mary C. Norment, *The Lowie History*, pp. 28-29, reprint p. 109.

Sgt. Bell, like his ancestor, Samuel Bell, is indeed proud to be a citizen of America. He is honored and privileged to have dutifully defended America against her enemies. Lastly, he is mighty proud of his Native American heritage given to him by his Progenitor, Pvt. Samuel Bell.

SUMMARY AND CONCLUSION

This writer in search for a marriage license for Samuel Bell (May 1749-Sep 1835) to Elizabeth "Betsy" Gilbert in NC, failed to discovered such a document. Writer discovered Samuel Bell married Polly Benson, Guilford County, NC.

However, in critical research searching Ancestry.com, censuses, birth, NC marriages, and death documents, writer did discover the marriage for Samuel Bell and Betsy Gilbert (1790-1864), 24 Apr 1806, Hancock, GA., by Samuel Dent, JP. Samuel's parents were: Col. Erasmus Thaddeus Beall, who served in the Revolutionary War and, Amelia Jane Beall, not Bell. Samuel and Betsy resided in Hancock, GA. Yet, writer did find evidence that a Betsy Gilchrist's name was associated to the Pvt. Samuel Bell descends in the Saddletree Community. More research is required.

In 1850, Bird Gilbert (abt. 1880, age, 70), VA, lived with Samuel and Betsy Gilbert Beall. Samuel was listed as a merchant. He was born in NC. Bird Gilbert married Sally Spinks. He served in the Civil War through GA Infantry, CO F, 3rd Regular. At his death, he was buried in the Gilbert Family Cemetery, Toomsboro, GA.[43]

The Samuel Bell descendants wish to pay tribute and honor and to celebrate their ancestor by placing a Revolutionary War grave marker near Hardy Holmes Bell grave marker in the Ten Mile Center Baptist Church Cemetery, Lumberton, NC.

[43] The Gilbert Family Cemetery, Toomsboro, GA, Ancestry.com: accessed.

The Bell and the Saddletree Colored Church Connection

In 1873, the leaders of the Methodist Episcopal Church, South (MECS) removed all forty-one "non-white" members' name from their church roll. Also, the Hammons gave the property to build the early "Hammon Church" on Stage Road, Lumberton, NC. The Hammon's church holds the earliest church deed in Robeson County. The "Hammons Church" list of Indian names were quickly stricken from the church membership roll.

According to the NC United Methodist Conference (NCCUMC) historian, Grill, wrote that the leaders in the "Saddletree Colored Church" consisted of the following individual: William N. [Nelson] Carter, who married Helen [Revels], 24 Nov 1855. They were grantors of the church. William Carter's second marriage was to Rona or Rena Smith, 8 Aug 1882.

Those serving as Trustees were: Hugh Smith; Neill Revels married Catherine Locklear, 6 Nov 1855; His second marriage was to Maria Bowen, 8 Jun 1860; Hinson Revels (10 Apr 1840-5 Mar 1890) married Sallie Deas [McGlocĐton], (1850-2 Mar 1922); burial in the Revels Cemetery; David Carter; and, Thomas Goins. David [Daniel] Carter (1830-1892) married Caroline Smith (10 Mar 1838-2 Feb 1920), 29 Nov 1856. Thomas Goins (1852) was the son of [William] James Goins (1835) and Vicy "Vissy/Vicie" Jones Locklear (1836) married 2 Nov 1851.

Sallie Deas father was John McGlocton. Caroline Smith Carter was buried in the Antioch Baptist Church Cemetery, Lumberton, NC.

Thomas Goins married Arona Carter, the daughter of William Carter and Helen Revels. Thomas was a relative to Minnie Goins (Jan 1887-1969), the daughter of Sarah Goins (1849). Minnie married Rev. Golden Andrew Carter.

According to the Revels Family history, the descendants of the Revels, Bells, Carters, and other members who were forced to leave the Saddletree Meeting House founded another church. According to the NC Methodist Conference historian another early church was the Thessalonica Church charted abt. 1792. The church deed for Thessalonica was deeded in 1880.

The Franklin Grill historical records signify that The Rev. Jeremiah Norman of the Bladen Charge preached at the Thessalonica meeting place on, 6 Nov 1800. The church doors were closed around 1939 after a long history of serving the Robeson County Indians. The church, was one among the oldest Indian churches in the Saddletree area. [ADDRESS FOR PRIVATE USE]

The results of the new North Carolina Constitution of 1835 caused disfranchising of "Free People" or "People of Color" which forbade them to bear arms. The Disfranchisement Law brought about far-reaching negative changes for "Free Persons of Color" in Robeson County. Such as the denial of their political and civic freedom and the removal of Indians beyond the Mississippi River. Again, it seemed there was no hope, despair swept across the face of the Indians. The Indians were deprived of an established church or churches in which to worship, nor could the Indian children continue to attend White schools.

In 1862, according to the NC Robeson County Circuit there were 124 members at the Saddletree Church. Purdie Locklear [Lowrie] and Jordan Chavis were two class leaders. While William Hammond served as the steward. William married Sallie Jane Jones. Jordan Chavis was the son of John Chavis and Eliza Revels. Jordan Chavis married Ella Frances.

Historian Grill indicated that the above Carter names were also listed on the Saddletree "Colored Church" roll. The doors of the Thessalonica Church closed during the 1930's having served the Robeson County Indians in the Saddletree Community for some one-hundred and fifty (150) years.[44]

Elijah Revels, a member of those who were of the "separated out" from Saddletree Colored Church, known as the Hammon Church, began another congregation in the Burnt Island Community, northeast of Lumberton, NC. The group gathered in a brush harbor until the first church, now known as the Antioch Baptist Church was founded. Antioch is known as the "Mother Church."

This writer has queries regarding the correct dates for the Thessalonica Church. If the church was charted abt. 1792, the church land was not deeded until 1880, who were the former members and where was the church located in the span of eighty-eight (88) years? As stated above, the Thessalonica Church is listed among the historical churches in the North Carolina United Methodist Church (NCCUMC) historical conference books.

In the following pages, this writer has compiled the name of persons who were those "separated out" from Saddletree Colored Church, as well as the Hammon Church. Many of the above soldiers listed in the essay and their families listed in this project attended the Saddletree Church and the Hammon Church and perhaps were buried in the Christian Cemetery. Such names as the Willises, Humphries, Blounts, and others, including slaves.

According to the Cumberland Marriage census, Hardy Bell married Sarah Parker, 1820. However, writer discovered that Sarah was also listed as Sallie Porter living in Columbus County, NC. Could she have been Sallie Porter who married Comp Porter (d. 1919)? No doubt, Sallie Porter was a sister or the mother to Priscilla Portee/Porter (1810). Priscilla married John Portee (1795). The family lived in Marion County, SC.

Hardy Bell and Sallie Porter's son was Amos Bell. According to Amos Bell's NC Death Certificate his parents were: Hardy Bell (1770-1867; Alt. 28 Apr 1866) and Sallie Porter, not Sarah Parker which could be an error in transcribing. Or, as she was known by family members during the enumerator's

---

[44] Bumgarner, George William, *Methodist Episcopal Church in North Carolina 1865-1939*, Hunter Publishing Company, Winston-Salem, NC 27113, USA, 1900., pp. 230-231].

visit. Hardy Bell and members of his immediate family were buried in the Ten Mile Cemetery, Lumberton, NC.

Nevertheless, Hardy Bell and Sarah Parker's children were: Mary Eliza, who married Nelson Smith [Carter], 16 Dec 1836; Amos Bell (d. 8 Feb 1919) married Catherine Revels, 14 Aug 1866; Cemore [Seemore] Bell married Eliza Hammons, 30 Mar 1854; and, Wiley Bell married Martha Ann Conner, 8 Mar 1854. And, William Andrew "Ander" Bell married Maggie Locklear, 10 Oct 1899.

Amos and Catherine Revels Bell's children were: Nancy, Duncan, Melendy, Ellen, Semore, and Warren Bell.

In 1844, Hardy Bell was the owner of 1594 acres of land in the Saddletree Community. Grady Locklear's resource states that Hardy Bell was a large land owner with 1797 acres taxed in the Saddletree Community.

Hugh Smith (12 Mar 1866-2 Jun 1947) married Orrie [Orra] Revels (1835-15 Feb 1920), 13 Oct 1835. His parents were: Nelson Smith and Eliza Bell. Eliza's parents were: Hardy Bell (1770) and Sarah Parker (1800). Orrie's parents were: Owen Revels (1804-1882) and Dorcas Hammond. Dorcas filed for her dower, 24 Mar 1882.

Another Orra was the daughter of Nathaniel Revels and Mary Elizabeth Lowrie. Their additional children were: Jonathan (1827-1872) married Nancy Bell (1836-1866); Frederick "Fred;" Malcolm; Helen; and, Henson [Hinson]. In the 1850 Robeson County census they were living in the household of Stephen and Vicy Lamb.

Henson [Hinson] Revels married Sarah Ann "Sallie" Deese. Frederick (1827-1 Oct 1902) married Frances Hardin (1837-1890). His second wife was Jane "Jeannie" Goins (1868-?), 27 Dec 1900. And, Lavia Revels (1835-1913), a sister, never married according to the Woriax Family history and Pvt. Samuel Bell family history. Nathaniel Revels' second marriage was to Helen Scott, Cumberland County, 17 Aug 1839.

According to the US Federal Census Mortality Schedules, 1850-1885, Nathaniel Revels (age 70, abt. 1799, NC), died September 1869. He was listed as a Pauper. Cause of death, accidently poisoned (NKA), Hillsboro Township, Orange County, NC. Also, James Griffin "Jim" Oxendine, Sr., (1793-25 Dec 1856) was listed on the Mortality Schedules.[45]

[45] Cummings-Woriax, *Creation*, p. 547.

Elizabeth Revels (1796-23 Sep 1873) married James Griffin "Jim" Oxendine, Sr., (1793-25 Dec 1856; his grave marker date (1821-16 Dec 1896), abt. 1816. James' parents were: Charles and Margaret Mainer Oxendine. His second wife was Elizabeth Lowry (14 Jun 1819-17 Nov 1889). James Griffin Oxendine served in the 1812 War.

In 1895, Griffin Oxenden "Oxendine" applied for Enrollment in Five Civilized Tribes. His enrollment was overturned as reported in the 1895 Dawes applications.

Hardy Holmes Bell married Narcissus "Sis" Hammons (10 Aug 1861-19 Nov 1933), 21 Mar 1878. Her parents were: George Washington Hammon [Hammonds] and Caroline Carter. Narcissus' brother was Rev. Stephen Andrew "S. A." Hammonds whose daughters were: Lela Jane and Docia. Lela Jane Hammonds (14 Jun 1905-4 Feb 1999) married John J. Brooks (12 Jan 1900-17 Dec 1960). And, Docia Hammonds (8 Jul 1900-1 Aug 1972) married Charlie Hammonds.

Charlie Hammonds' parents were: H. B. Canady and Jane Revels. Narcissus and Hardy Holmes Bell's daughter, Hattie Bell (3 Sep 1901-5 Oct 2000) married Grady Canady, 4 Sep 1919. Grady Canady's second marriage was to Fannie Bell (7 Jun 1912-12 Aug 1960).

Hattie and Grady's son, Tilman married Lydia. Tilman Canady was murdered, 21 Sep 1947.

Clarifia [Clarisy Chavis] Isreal married Hardy Revels, 15 Jan 1845, Robeson County. Hardy's parents were: Gabriel Revels (1819-1883) and Annie Jane Lowry (1820), Sampson County, NC. Gabriel's trade was a self-employed shoe-maker. No doubt, Clarisy was formerly Clarissa Bell.

Claifia's parents were: Jonathan Revells (1822-1872) and Nancy Bell (1836-1866; alt. date 1825-2 Mar 1922), 11 Oct 1943. Jonathan's parents were: Nathaniel Sampson Revels and Mary Elizabeth "Sallie" Lowrie. According to the Woriax-Revels family tree, Nathaniel's first wife was Nancy Edith Manior [Maynor], Sampson County. No doubt, she was a member of the Josiah Manier and Elizabeth Lousia Lee family, Sampson County, NC.

Nancy Edith's sibling, Pvt. Josiah Manier, Jr., (1839-15 Aug 1862), served in the Confederacy, Company H., Regiment 20th Infantry.

Revells, Jonathan (1822-1872), enlisted in the Civil War as a Confederate soldier. His parents were: Nathaniel Sampson Revels and Mary Elizabeth Lowery. Jonathan married Nancy Bell (1836-1866). Was Nancy Bell a member of Samuel Bell's family?

Samuel Revels married Charity Oxendine, 8 Mar 1860.

Jonathan and Nancy Bell's son, Jonathan Revels, Jr., (1842-6 Aug 1917), served in the Civil War as a Confederate soldier. The Revels members who left the Saddletree Church established another church in the Saddletree Community [Burnt Island] known as Antioch.

Another church member, Nancy Jane Caps' [Capps] whose mother was Elizabeth Copps (White), formerly of Island Creek, Duplin County, NC. Nancy Jane married John W. Sampson, 23 Dec 1853. They lived in Brunswick County. John W. (1833), served in the Confederate Army through Brunswick County, Wilmington, NC. Writer discovered another, Samuel Bell living in Brunswick County.

Writer discovered while reading Records of Estates, Warren County, NC, Col. 1, 1780-1805, by David B. Gammon, 1988, the following names, Nancy Capps [an orphan of Francis Capps] bound to Wm. Capps, Aug. Ct., 1810. And, Hicksey Capps [age 7, orphan of Francis Capps] bound to Silus [Silas] Capps, Aug. Ct., 1810.

In addition to Rhoda Carter who was bound to Thomas Shearin. In the Cumming-Woriax *Creation*. Shearin [Sheridan] married Lucy Oxendine, Robeson County, NC. Sheridan was a Civil War soldier who later became a merchant in Robeson County and Bladen County, NC.

Sheridan, Thomas (1788-1864), Pvt., served as a Fifer through Capt. Jacob Hartman Company, NC Militia in the 1812 War. He married Lucy Oxendine, 17 Dec 1851. After, his discharged Thomas was a merchant in Bladen County. Lucy received his pension.

Lucy and Thomas' children were: Atlas, Condary, and Selas. No doubt, they gave their son the name Selas as a namesake for the above Silus [Silas] Capps.

Henry H. Sampson (1804-1874) married Nancy Carter (1802-1897). Their son, William Sampson (27 Mar 1832-1 Aug 1909), was the father of Oscar Sampson (17 Jan 1866-9 Jan 1978). Oscar married Susie Jane Oxendine (21 Nov 1916-7 May 1925). Their daughter, Ruth Sampson (19 Jun 1897-21 Jan 1929) and Winnie Lee Bell, the daughter of Rev. John and Serena Bell, were recognized as the first two Indian women to earn a four-year high school diploma from the early Normal School, Pembroke, NC, now known as the University of North Carolina at Pembroke.

After graduation, Ruth attended Carson College in TN. Ruth returned to Pembroke. She married Willie Sanford Locklear. Ruth taught in the Indian schools in Robson County. Ruth and her parents were buried in the Sampson Cemetery.

In critical research this writer discovered Timothy Locklear (2 Dec 1841-29 May 1919), John Hardin (1848), and Titus Locklear (1843) living with John A. Barnes in the 1850 Brunswick, GA census. Also, others listed on the census were: Isaac Taylor; Nelly Revels; Helen Revels (1837-1912) married William Nelson Carter (1835-15 Sep 1889/1899); Caroline Carter (1839-1930); Owen Revels (1799); Dorcas Hammonds (1797); Susan; Hinson; and, Orra Revels, who married Hugh Smith. Hinson married Sarah Ann "Sallie" Deese. Owen Revels and Dorcas Hammonds were married 23 Apr 1831.

Nelson Carter married Roma Smith, 1832.

Timothy was reared by Stephen Barnes, house #704, Robeson County. John A. Barnes served as a postmaster, Robeson County and served as a physician during the Civil War. Timothy Locklear, alias Fun Allen Locklear, married Anne Eliza Dial (2 Dec 1862-29 May 1919). Fun Allen's parents were: Needham Locklear (1788-1868, age 80) and Mariah [Moriah] Locklear (1800-1889, age 89). It is apparent that both Fun Allen and Anne Eliza's death dates are the same date. Perhaps, both died during the great flu epidemic in 1919. More research is required.

Could Titus Locklear be Fun Allen's sibling? Thomas "T" Locklear married Mary Revels, 25 Oct 1883.

Apparently, Needham and Mariah Locklear had lived together as man and wife until their marriage. According to their marriage certificate, 11 Aug

1866/1868, Needham was (80) years-of-age and Mariah (89) years-of-age. They were buried in the Hamie Bullard Cemetery, Wild Cat Dr., Prospect Community, Maxton, NC.

Needham's maternal grandparents were: Jerry Prevatt and Rosa Ann Monroe (abt. 1841-1915, age 74), the daughter of Roaxanna [Roxan "Ciss"] Monroe. In 1856, Joseph Bruce brought charges against Needham. Needham was charged $1.20 warrant fee.

[The above sections of families were adapted from Cummings-Woriax's book, *The Creation of An Innovative People 1700-1887: The Shaping of a New Territory, Robeson County, NC*, pp. 161-162.]

The following names were members of newly formed Antioch Church, "the Mother Church," who served in the Revolutionary War:

William Burd [Byrd], Thomas Hester, Milbea Musselwhite, John Parker, Francis Parker, Joel Pitman, John Purnell, Henry Taylor, I., and Henry Taylor, II. [Presented to writer by the Antioch Baptist Church Historian.]

Members and others connected to Samuel Bell's family attended the Saddletree Colored Church

Non-White Members "separated out" from Saddletree Colored Church, formerly known as Hammond, December 5, 1873.

Purdie Locklear	Doras Revels
William Hammond	Maria Revels
Jordan Chavis	Phillip Locklear
Malcolm Revels	Clarifia Chavis
Wm Locklear	Amos Bell
Samuel Revels	Needham Locklear
Hugh Smith	Wm. Santee
Fred Revels	Christian Locklear
Henson Revels	Florida Chavis
Elizabeth Revels	Nancy Revels
Susan Revels	Sallie Ann Revels
Charia Locklear	Eliza Chavis
Winnie Locklie	Priscilla Portee
Lavinia Revels	Susan Locklear
Orra Smith	Kitty Hammond
Helen Carter	Nancy Jane Caps
Susan Oxendine	Sarah Smith
David Carter	Eloa Hammond
William Carter	Charia Lowrie
Helen Santee	Aries Monroe
	Sarah N. Oxendine

*[Note: Spelling of original names may have suffered corruption in Scottish translation.]

[Extracted from Carolyn Cummings-Woriax's Hood Theological Seminary Doctoral Project, May 2013.]

Sarah "Sally" Santee Teeter (22 Aug 1796-2 Jan 1876).

[Photo extracted from DuarteK59 24 May 2016, Ancestry.com accessed: 31 May 2017.]

Sarah "Sally" Santee Teeter's father was John Santee. Sarah married: Samuel B. Teeter [Tetter], (4 Jul 1796). At their marriage 20 Jan 1820, Samuel stated he was 21 years-of-age. Writer discovered a younger Sarah Tetter (20 May 1856). Writer failed to discover her relationship to John Santee. In 1850, Samuel Tedder [Tetter] was head of (4) Household Members living in Bladen County, NC.[46]

No doubt, Samuel Tedder was a member of writer's (5x) great-grandmother, Winnie Tetter who married Enoch Cummins. Winnie's father was Revolutionary War soldier, Pvt. Mores [Morris] Teader [Tetter], (1737-1812). Morris Tetter was buried in the Cummins Family Cemetery formerly known as Bee Branch Cemetery, Union Chapel Rd., Pembroke, NC.

---

[46] Cummings-Woriax, *Creation*, p. 312.

Hardy Holme's England Record Image

Hardy Holmes's Grave Marker Image

Hardy Holmes's wife, Fereba Moore's family Grave Marker Image

Writer visited the Thompson-Moore Cemetery, 9 Oct 2019. The above Image 3 and 4 - First Lt. Hardy Holmes (1750-14 Jul 1828) Grave Marker and the Moore Family Grave Marker, Turkey, Sampson County, NC.

Which Hardy Holmes Died 11 Sep 1819? *Clarification*: In Deed Book 12, p. 161, George Holmes' deed to William Holmes is for his interest in land that fell to him by heirship from his father, Hardy Holmes, deceased, Sep. 11, 1819.

In Turkey, NC at Cabin Museum Road and the railroad crossing is the Historical Marker for Thomas Overton Moore (10 Apr 1804-25 Jun 1876), Sampson County. He served in various wars; lived with an uncle in Louisiana who taught him the trade of a planter in Louisiana. He lived a successful life as a planter and served in politics. Thomas was elected Governor of Louisiana. At his death Thomas Overton Moore was buried in the Mt. Olivette Cemetery,

Pineville, LA. No doubt, Moore was a member of the Moore family who continue to live in the Sampson County area.

Names Adapted from the NC Indian Revolutionary War List.

BELL, SAMUEL, Lumbee Indian "other free", S6598 [born May 1749 in Surry Co. VA], RNC:454, OLIK, enl. Robeson Co., res. Duplin Co. [Note: DAR established patriot.]

CARTER, JOHN EDWARD, **, R10316, Duplin Co.

CARTER, MOSES, African American, 1790 NC ("Other Free"), S41470, HEI 2, Cumberland Co.

HAMMOND, ISAAC, African American ("Free Negro"), W7654 [married Dicey in Fayetteville in 1787; he died 1822; she died October 10, 1852; daughter Rachel, son George], RNC:134, HEI 2, Cumberland Co.

HAMMOND, JOHN, Mixed descent ("Lumbee Indian" or "Mulatto"), S8654 [died October 1858], OLIK, 1850 NC Robeson Co., Anson Co.

LOMACK, WILLIAM, African American, 1790 NC ("Other Free"), S41783, a son, Enock Lomack.

MANUEL, JESSE, African American, 1790 NC ("Other Free"), S41808, McBRIDE4:XIII:93, HEI 2, Bladen Co.

The above is an example as to how the early US American Military Armed Forces listed Indian soldiers. Most were seldom listed as Indians. Writer in her research discovered that many were listed "other free," "mulatto," or "Free Negro." Research for a list of American Indian soldiers proved to be most difficult. At their enlistments, many were erroneously identified due to the different complexion hues of American Indians; the early corruption of surname spelling; and those who had moved and no longer lived in these local areas which were then often listed as White.

BOOK II

REVOLUTIONARY WAR PATRIOT
JOHN BROOKS

BROOKES OR BROOKS

The surname is thought be derived from residing near a stream or brook. English, Gaelic, and Scottish, possessive case of Brook [of the brook] Old English *broc*

Older Brooks Descends oral tradition:

John Brooks lived in Johnston County, death Johnston County, NC; burial unknown.

Older Brooks knew him as "Pappy;" a sailor, "sailed on the queen ships;" came through Savannah, GA; and, his heritage- European and French and/or European and Waccamaw Siouan.

Front Cover Crest/Shield Legend

Feathers – Indian Heritage and Life

Old Field – former Indian villages

Sea Anchor – sailed on Queen's ships

Dogwood – North Carolina State flower

Jail Bars - Prisoner of War, Florida

Gun - Militia Musket or Military Rifle

The Crest/Shield was designed to capture John Brooks' known life events.

*Crest/Shield Designer: Rev. Dr. Carolyn Cummings-Woriax, 2017

*Free Hand Pencil Artist: Eric Woriax, 2018

JOHN BROOKS S6732 REVOLUTIONARY WAR SOLDIER

- (1757- 4 September 1863)

- Day and month of Birth – unknown

- Place of Birth - unknown

- Parents: unknown

- Place of Death and Burial – unknown, assumed Robeson County, NC

- John Brooks married Pattie "Paty" Lowrie (1795-15 Aug 1867)

- Daughter of William Lowrie and Elizabeth "Bettie" Locklear

- No marriage record discovered

- William Lowrie served as a soldier in the Whigs and Tories War and as a Revolutionary War Soldier

- John Brooks and Pattie Lowrie's Children:

- Rolen [Rowland or Roland], Harriet, and Miata Minta "Mittie" Brooks

- James John Brooks (1758-d. 1828, Butts, GA)

- Revolutionary War Soldier, believed to be a relative to John Brooks.

- James lived in Fayetteville, Cumberland County, NC, died in Georgia.

Other Brooks associated to John Brooks

- Jesse Brooks [married] listed in Bladen County Tax List, 1774. Betty Brooks listed in the Bladen County Tax List and 1790 Robeson County census as Head of (4) Household Members.

Unknown Brooks

- Jesse (SC, 1800), Keziah (1805), Ellaner (1765), her granddaughter, Lendy Locklear, Rachel Brooks (1764), Christian (1820), and Celia (1823). Court records reveal that Celia [Caty or Scilly] died before her husband Hector Locklear's divorce became final.

- Ellaner Brooks and John Brooks are listed in the Vestry Book of St. Peter's Parish 1684-1786, New Kent County, VA, p. 718.

Land Record of Deeds FFF, 774 & 775.

Rowland Brooks & wife [Henrietta], Philip Locklear & wife [Mittie Locklear] and Harriet Graham. Land deeds the Brooks heirs and Philip Locklear.

On page 368, #3, NC Wills and Probate Records, 1665-1998 for John Brooks, states that John Brooks died in Sep 1863... and since the death of his widow [no name given].

On page 368, #4, the Plaintiff [Roland] Rowland Brooks, Mittie Jones, and Harriet Graham, the children and only heirs at law of the said John Brooks.

Land Warrant Number 80030, 160 acres, Robeson County, NC.

John Brooks, abt. ninety-six years-of-age, applied for his military pension. The application was executed 30 May 1853. Pattie "Paty" Lowrie Brooks sought her dower of the John Brooks' heir estate in 1863.

INTRODUCTION:

This writer in her critical research contacted Prof. Malinda Maynor Lowery, a direct descendant of the John Brooks and Pattie Lowrie's family. Malinda is a professor at the University of North Carolina at Chapel Hill, NC. In her book, *Race, Identity, & The Making of A Nation: Lumbee Indians in the Jim Crow South*, appendices listed four (4) Genealogy Charts illustrating the Locklear, Brooks, Lowrie, and Oxendine family's tree. The second chart focuses on the Brooks genealogy reference of John Brooks as the progenitor of the Brookes or Brooks in Robeson County, NC.

It has been suggested that John Brooks was married three times or was the father of three different families. Writer failed to discover any marriage records for John Brooks. John Brooks and Pattie Lowrie were listed as the parents of Roland Brooks who died in 1886. Roland, Rolin, or Rowland was told by relatives that he was the son of John Brooks and Pattie Lowry Brooks.

Hector Brooks, the son of Roland, stated that his mother was Betsy Patsy "Tempsy" Locklear Brooks (1826-1877), 6 May 1834. Roland later married Betsy Locklear (1826-1877), the former wife of Elijah Jones (1816-1860 alt. date 25 Aug 1857), 27 May 1844. Following her marriage to Roland Brooks, Betsy changed her children's surnames from Jones to Brooks.

Philip Jones Locklear's mother was Matilda Jones, a member of the Elijah Jones family.

Hector Brooks [one of the "Original 22"] testimony was extracted from "Applicant #64 (Hector Brooks) in Carl Seltzer, 'A Report on the Racial Status of Certain People in Robeson county, North Carolina.'"[47]

---

[47] Cummings-Woriax, Brooks Family History, National Archives and Records Administration, Record Group 75, Entry 616, Box 14/15—North Carolina, March 3, 2018.

John Brooks Family #1

John was believed to be the son of John Brooks and Lovedy Locklear.

I. John "Jack" Brooks, Jr., (SC, 1824 and/or NC, 1828) married Betsy "Bettie" or Beady Locklear (1840), 27 Feb 1846. Beady Locklear's parents were: Aaron Locklear and Sabra Manuel/Emmanuel, Sampson County, NC. Aaron's parents were: James Cricket Locklear and Rhoda Quick, SC.

A. John "Jack" and Beady Locklear's Children:
   1. Joseph "Joe" Brooks married Charity Jones. His second wife was Susan (NKA).
   2. Jesse "Jess B." Brooks married Vercilla Lowrie, 23 Jul 1895. She was the daughter of Irving [Ervin] Lowrie (1838). He was a half-brother to Calvin "Fent" Lowrie. In the 1920 census an infant grandson, Brooks Lowery (11/12), and Nancy Lowry, age 18, a daughter-in-law were listed as members of Calvin Fent's family.
   3. Lovedy Brooks (1858-14 Feb 1949) married John David Locklear (1850-25 Jun 1935). Lovedy's grave marker reads "Lovedy Brooks (1849-1949)." John David was the son of Archibald Locklear "Big Arch" (1829-21 Jan 1904) married Elizabeth "Betsy" Lowrie (1838). Their daughter was Beadie Ann, death Burke County, 3 Apr 1960.
   4. Christian Brooks (1865-15 Jan 1933) married Nathaniel Locklear.
   5. Dockery Brooks (NC, Apr 1866- 12 Feb 1930, GA) married Cal-

lie Jones [Campbell/Locklear], (May 1868-1 Sep 1929), 29 Jul 1879. Virginia "Ginny" Graham accompanied the couple to Dillon, SC where they were married.

6. Aaron Brooks (1852) married Dalsedia "Della" Locklear (1855 1930). Dalcede Brooks NC Death Certificate states her death, 10 Jul 1937. She was (92) years of age. Her parents: Archibald Locklear and Martha Locklear Cummings.

Aaron and Dalsedia's (13) Children:

Rutherford [Ralph or Pikey] Brooks, Lawson Brooks, Zack Brooks, Rachel Brooks married Isaiah Locklear, John Rowland Brooks, Colan Brooks married Mary Dial, Lillie J. Brooks (1863) married June Brooks, second marriage Elisha Locklear (1883), Rosetta Brooks, Ruthie Ann Brooks, Mary Lee Brooks married James Hammons, Dougald Brooks, Fannie Brooks married Owen Jacobs, and Ida [Lee] Brooks married Chavis. Ida's daughter was Minnie Chavis. Ida Lee's second marriage was to Huel Locklear, SC. [48] (Extracted from Land Deed 6 T, p.175, Robeson County Courthouse Land Deeds,13 Apr 2016). Aaron was buried in the Brooks family cemetery.

3a. Lillie Jane Brooks and Elisha Locklear's son, Elisha Locklear is an oral historian and artist.

Lillie Jane and Elisha' daughter, Dalsedia (1912) was shot and killed, 19 Nov 1955 by Sam Junior Brooks (19 Oct-17 Jul 1971). Sam's parents were: John Slater Brooks and Maggie Jacobs. Maggie's parents were: Sam Jacobs and Annie.

3b. Zachariah "Zack" Brooks married Martha Mae "Mollie" (1896). Zack Brooks was the founder of the Harpers Ferry Baptist Church.

Christian "Christine" Brooks (1820-1805) and Nathan Walden (d.1849) were the parents of "Jack or Zack" Brooks (1805), SC. Christian was thought to be the mother of John Brooks, Jr. If she was the mother of John Brooks, Jr., there is a conflict in ages according to John's 1824 birthdate, Christian's birthdate, and Zack Brooks year of birth.

---

[48] Extracted from Aaron Brook's Land Deed 6 T, p.175, Robeson County Courthouse Land Deeds, 13 Apr 2016.

John Brooks Family #2

Peggy Locklear was the daughter of James "Cricket" Locklear and Rhoda Quick, SC. She was a sister to Aaron Locklear.

II. John Brooks and Peggy Locklear's Children:
  A. Bessie [Betsy or Patsy] Locklear married Neil [Elijah] Jones, 27 May 1844.
    1. Their daughter Callie Jones (1868) married Dockery Brooks 1866). Their children were:
      1a. David Junior Brooks.
      1b. Will Brooks married Leanna Locklear (1895-Apr 1971), who was one of the "Original 22." Will served in the US Army, WWI, as a Medic. Will and Leanna were buried in the National Cemetery, Gettysburg, PA.

Note: The community in which both Brooks-Locklear families lived and continue to live is known as the Tuscarora Indian Settlement. Early Land Records suggest the areas was known as the Brooks Swamp. It has been suggested that the Brooks settlement was a closed community for about 100 years.

John Brooks Family #3

Clarification: Discrepancy in age: Pattie "Paty" Lowrie (1795-15 Aug 1867), and Roland Brooks (1814). The discrepancy arises in Pattie and Roland's birthdates. If Roland was the son of John Brooks, then he was the product of another woman, or the son of John Brooks' former wife, but not Pattie's son. Or, another possibility is an error in Pattie's recorded birth year. Perhaps, William Lowrie [Loughery], (1750/1758-28 May 1847), Revolutionary War soldier, and Betty Locklear's children were older than their recorded birthdates. Nonetheless, William's son, Allen Lowrie's death date disputes this hypothesis due to the fact at his death, 9 Mar 1865; his grave marker reads that he was (70) years of age. This confirms Allen Lowrie was born abt. 1790/1795.

In the 1800 Robeson County census, John Brooks was listed as Head of (7) Household Members. In the 1800 Bladen County census, William Lowrie, father of Patty, was listed as Head of (5) Household Members. William's household, no doubt, was extended Lowrie member's children.

Second, reviewing Hopewell Holiness Methodist Church history and Cummings-Brooks family resources, it is recorded that William Lowrie, **did not marry** "Betty" Locklear until after the death of his father, James Lowrie, in 1811. Reviewing James [G his mark] Lowrie's 1810 Last Will and Testament, Betty Locklear's father, Bennet [Localare] Locklear, s/by X mark as a testator to James Lowrie's will. Bennet Localare served in the Revolutionary War, Warren County, NC.

Third, references have suggested William Lowrie married "Cele." James Lowrie's youngest daughter was "Cele" or "Selah" the sole heir of his estate. Writer failed to discovered validated claims that William married a woman with the name, Cele.

Fourth, Susan Locklier, March 1853, made application for William's military pension stating that she and William Loughery were married in 1803. Writer believes Esther Lowrie (1810-1906) who married Jordan Oxendine could possibly be William and Susan's daughter. Writer failed to discover documentation to support this theory.

III. John Brooks and Pattie "Paty" Lowrie Children:

Roland, Harriet, and [Miata] Minta "Mittie" Brooks
    Roland Brooks (1807/1815-1886) married Henrietta Betty Patsy Locklear (1826-1877), alias Tempsy Brooks, 6 May 1834. Tempsy's mother was: Margaret Locklear. At (60) years-of-age, Roland married Betty "Betsy" Locklear (1851, 28 years-of-age), 29 Jul 1879. Witnesses were: Philip Jones, Charity Jones, and Elias Oxendine. Betsy was formerly married to Elijah Jones. She changed her children's surname from Jones to Brooks after her marriage to Roland Brooks. This is confirmed by Robeson County censuses.

    A. Roland and Betsy's Children:
        1. John Hector Brooks (1862-1950) married Nancy Jane Locklear (7 Aug 1865-28 May 1947), 2 Apr 1866. Her parents were: Whitfield (1830-7 Jun 1915) and Flora Locklear (1845-20 Jul 1910). Flora's parents were: Daniel and Hillary Locklair. Hector stated that he had one full brother, Slater Brooks and two sisters (both died).

John and Nancy's Children:
        1a1 Jennie (20 Jun 1887-16 May 1968), Frances (20 Nov 1888-20 Oct 1960), Wilson (1890-22 Dec 1951), Garfield (1892), Tracie (1896-?), Flora Jane (3 Jun 1906-10 Jan 1997), Mary Lee (21 Jul 1912-30 May 1913), and O'quinn (1887-1975).

1a1a. O'quinn Brooks married Catherine "Bertha" Locklear (1906-1953) a member of the James B. Locklear and Lucinda Swett family.

O'Quinn and Catherine's Children:
1a1b. Katherine (25 Aug 1923-15 Dec 2012) married James H. Dial. Their children were: James Hector, Eugene, Cleveland, and Mary.
1a1c. Gerald Brooks married Jacobs.

John Hector Brooks and Annie Elizabeth Lowry's son, Henry Clayton Brooks. John Hector Brooks' brother, John Slater Brooks, also known as Jess B. [Jesse] Brooks.

2. John Slater Brooks (1860) was a half-brother to Calvin F. "Fent" Lowry (Sep 1858-22 May 1933), the son of Rose Zelda Lowry. Calvin married Mary M. McAllister (SC, 1867-1931), the daughter of Margaret Locklear.

Calvin Fent's siblings: Jesse Brooks, Irving Lowry, Johnnie Oxendine, and Flora Locklear Oxendine.

Irving Lowry [Ervin], (d. 16 Jan 1919, 83 years-of-age) married Flora Locklear, the daughter of Daniel and Hillary Locklair. Irving's parents were: Alfred Locklear Lowry (1811-1848). Alfred married Isabella Elizabeth Locklear Lowrie (1819), 1835. Alfred's mother was Elizabeth "Betty" Locklear who married William Lowrie. William adopted Alfred Locklear. Betty's parents were: Bennet Locklear and Elizabeth Locklear.

John Slater married Mary Maggie Jacob (1864-1942), 2 Apr 1910. She was the daughter of Sam Jacobs (1842) and Annie (1848).

2a1. John Slater and Maggie's Children:
2a1a. Maggie Lee (14 July 1923)
2b. John Slater and Maggie's Children:
2b1. Sam Junior Brooks (19 Oct 1900-17 Jul 1971). Sam married Hattie Mae Locklear also known as Allie "Annie," 19 Nov 1955. Sam shot and killed younger, Dalcidy Locklear (1910-19 Nov 1955). Her parents were: Elisha Locklear and Lillie J. Brooks.

2b1a. Bowman Brooks married Lorene Cummings, the daughter of Julius "Jule" Cummings and Eva Mae Clark. Jule's mother was Winnie Cummings, the daughter of Elisha Cummings and Mary Locklear, SC.

2b2. Pearlie Lee Brooks (SC, 8 Sep 1913-1998) married Robert "Buddy" Brayboy (22 Jul 1910-8 Jun1981).

2bc. John C. "Candy" Brooks (1920-?).

Harriet Brooks (1831-abt.1920/1930) married Duncan Graham (1795-1897). His first wife was Elizabeth Ausley. Duncan was a merchant and served as a postmaster. He was a brother to John N. Graham, the father of Virginia "Ginny" Graham.

A. Harriet and Duncan's Children:
1. Rachel, Frances, Sarah, Amanda, and Mary. Harriet's grandson, Duncan Graham married Dovie Lowry.
   1a Mary Graham married Archie Deese. Their children were: Gus and Hector Deese.
   1a1. Gus Deese's children were: John Garner, Louise, and others.
   1a2. Hector Deese's children were: Shaw and others.
   1b. Amanda Graham married Riley Oxendine. Riley's parents were: Michael James Cummings and Sarah Ann Oxendine. Michael was the son of the Isaac "Ike" Cummings and Elizabeth Swett Lowrie. Michael and Sarah Ann's Children: James Riley and John Henry Oxendine.
   1b1. James Riley Oxendine married Christian Graham. A member of the John N. Graham and Beda Locklear family.
   1b2. John Henry Oxendine married Effie Jane Brooks.

Harriet Brooks Graham married Linzey Locklear (1833-1903), 18 Apr 1897. Linzey was the son of Levi Locklear and Patsy Evans. Linzy's first wife was Anna Jane Locklear. Harriet and Linzey lived on the "Billy Booker Farm" near Curtis "Curt" and Catherine Locklear's home, near the University of North Carolina at Pembroke University campus. Catherine was the daughter of Rufus J. [Johnson] Locklear and Sophrina "Frannie" Revels. Rufus was a descend of the Enoch Cummins family.

   In the 1920 Robeson County census, Harriet chose to return to her former name, Harriet Graham.

2. Harriet and Lenzy's Children, None:
3. Lenzy's Children:
   3a. Leonard Locklear married Tilda. His daughter, Lennie Locklear Lowry was the mother of Curt Locklear and Monroe Lowry. Curt married Catherine Locklear.
   3a1.Curt and Catherine's Children: Janice, Cathy, Nancy, Curt, Jr., Milton, Stevie, Marcia, Lindsay, and Anthony.

Mittie Brooks (14 Jul 1835-9 May 1906) and [John] Joe Oxendine (SC, 1820-16 May 1897; alt. date 1915, NC), the son of Elias Oxendine.

C. Mittie and John Joe's Children:
   1. Alexander "Sandy" Brooks (15 Jul 1851-22 Feb 1943) was blind in his right eye. Sandy married Effie Jane Hunt (4 Apr 1861-10 Sep 1934), the daughter of Ollen "Orlen" Hunt (SC, 1830-18 Dec 1913) and Martha Hunt (1841-22 Mar 1921), descend of Progenitor Lewis Hunt. Sandy grew up in the home of Allen Lowrie and Mary "Polly" Cumbo. He and the following children Russel Lowrie, Mary Frances Lowrie, Phil Jones, and Henry Berry Lowrie were working in the field with Allen when he was charged with larceny. Both, Allen and his son, William, were tried in a mock court, sentenced to death, and executed, 9 Mar 1865. Sandy was listed as Sandy Loury in the 1870 census living with Polly Lowrie.

Alexander "Sandy" and Effie Jane's Children:
   Eliza, Edmond "Ed," James Ollen "Bud," Raymond, Elizabeth "Bettie," Malinda "Lindy," Andrew "Ander," Effie Jane, Margie, Little Sandy, Jr., John J., Peter "Pete," and Joseph "Joe."

   1a. Mary Eliza (28 Jul 1881-18 Mar 1948) married Alec Chesley Locklear (22 Nov 1879-29 Oct 1954).
       His parents: James "Mack" Locklear and Aggie Nora Hunt.
       Mary Eliza and Alec's Children:
       1a1.Aggie (1 Jul 1898-20 Sep 1982) married Hezzie Deese

(8 Jan 1899-3 Mar 1989), Carrie Lee, and Wallie (30 Jan 1905-27 Apr 1936).

Uncle Caswell Hunt (2 Feb 1865-30 Nov 1957), William Berry Strickland, Maggie Lena, and several grandchildren and other children lived in their home.

1b. Joseph Ollen "Bud" (11 Dec 1882-16 Oct 1964) married Noviller "Novella" Hunt (Apr 1885-abt.1905). Her parents were: John Noah Hunt and Mary Ann Oxendine.

Ollen and Novella's Children:
1b1. Leona (31 Aug 1905-15 Feb 2004) married Donnie Revels.
Ollen's second wife was Anna Hunt (2 Jun 1891-14 Sep 1977), the daughter of Dudley and Pirie Hunt (1881-1968), 13 Oct 1907.

Ollen and Anna's children:
1b2. Macie (1910) married Fred Chavis; Thelma (1914) married Norman Hammonds; Margaret (21 Feb 1925); James Ollen (16 Sep 1913-20 Jul 1928); and, Kenneth B. (7 Nov 1929-6 Jun 1969) married Juanita Odom. Margaret married (NKA) Chavis, and James Ollen never married.

1c. Raymond (24 Sep 1884-18 Apr 1948) married Carrie "Scrap" Hunt, 2 Sep 1907. It is believed she was murdered by a Lambert.
1c1. Raymond's second wife (NKA), per Van C. Locklear, Bessie and Bennet Locklear's son.
1c2. Raymond's third wife, Bessie Roller, SC.

Raymond and Bessie's Children:
1c2a. Mary Eliza (22 Jan 1922), Raymond, Jr., Martha, Margarette, Wilton (18 July 1934), and Samuel.

2c. Bessie married Bennet Locklear, a descend of elder Bennet Locklear, Revolutionary War soldier.
Bessie and Bennet's Children:
2c1a. Van Cephas Locklear (d. 2019).

1d. Elizabeth "Bettie" (4 Nov 1888-18 Oct 1947) married Allen Hunt, 7 May 1907.

Bettie and Allen's Children: [parents of 17 children]
1d1. Mary Margaret; Velma D.; Flora Bell married an Oxendine; Mable; Lorraine; Eula Mae; Alean married Elwood N. Oxendine; Josephine; Christine married Walker; Irene married Glenn Locklear; Allen Clifton; George Clyde; John Stanton; Wade B. Hunt; and, Howard. Neither Margaret, Lorraine, Eula Mae, Clifton, nor Mable ever married.

1e. Edmond "Ed" (18 Sep 1889-29 Jul 1948) married Martha Jane Swett (d. 1942). Her parents were: Rufus "Claude" Frank Swett and Maggie Owens, SC. Frank's parents were: [Frank] Eli and Nancy Swett/Sweat.

Edmond and Martha's Children:
1e1. Naomi (1907-1991) married Hudler Hunt (29 Mar 1905-20 Jan 1975); Edna (18 Sep 1909-18 May 1994) married James Ellsworth "Jim" Chavis (1895-1979); Percy (7 Jul 1911-11 Feb 1980) married Anna Cummings (25 May 1908-3 Sep 1988); Lettie Mae (24 Jul 1915-20 Jun 1966) married Bontford "BF" Cummings (30 May 1915-11 May 2004); Edmond Worth (26 Aug 1917-24 Jan 1986) married Dora Frances Chavis (25 May 1918-1991); Leotha (7 Feb 1921-20 Jun 1998) married Joseph "Buddy" Jacobs; and, Stella May (23 Oct 1922-) married Lawrence Locklear (1920-2003).

1f. Malinda "Lindy" (21 Mar 1890-14 Jun 1970) married John Chavis (16 Feb 1889-28 Mar 1919). His mother was Molinda Lambert. He was murdered near the Atlantic Coastline trestle, Pembroke, NC. He was a descend of the Pvt. Ishmel Chavis family.

Malinda and John's Children:

1f1. Ester; Effie Jane married Rev. Gold Carter; Hildreth married Foy Cummings; Willie; and, Nehemiah.

Malinda and her children lived with the Ed Brooks' family in the 1920's.
Malinda second husband was Dockery Locklear, 5 Feb 1920. No children were born.
Malinda's third husband was Gordon Dial. No children were born.

1g. Andrew Worth "Ander" (19 Nov 1882-4 Feb 1974) married Mary Jane Hunt, the daughter of Asbury "Berry" and Lucy Hunt Locklear.

Ander and Mary Jane's Children:

1g1. Venus (11 Sep 1914-13 Sep 1969) married Lucy Belle Wilkins; Worth (27 Feb 1917-17 Jun 2002) married Flora Margaret Locklear (3 Jun 1910-7 Oct 1990); Raymond "Jack" (28 Jun 1919- 4 Jun 2002); Harold (19 Sep 1924-12 Jun 1943); Emae Mae (11 Dec 1926-31 Aug 2014) married Ebert Locklear; James Andrew (22 May 1929-13 Jul 1958); Charles Roscoe (1 Mar 1932-9 Nov 1986); Lora Neal (d. 2016) married Willard Cummings (d. 2017); and, Betty Rose married Johnny Locklear.
Neither Jack nor Harold ever married.

1h. Effie Jane (1892-?) married John Henry Oxendine (15 Mar 1873-12 Mar 1948), 1915. His parents were: Michael James Cummings and Sarah Ann Oxendine. Michael's parents: Isaac "Ike" Cummings and Elizabeth "Eliza" Swett Lowrie.

1h1. Effie and John Henry's Children:
   Proctor; Martha Lee; Lou Ellen; Evelyn; Huey; J. W.;
   Gerald; and, Mary Jane married Cleveland Locklear.

1i. Margie married Shaw Deese (27 Oct 1895-19 Oct 1973), the
   son of Hector Deese and Luellen Oxendine. Hector Deese's
   parents were: Mary Graham and Archie Deese, SC.

Margie and Shaw's Children:

1i1. John D.; Margarette; Tommie; Herb; Margie Ellen;
   Charlie; and, Samuel "Sam."

1j. Alex, Jr., "Little Sandy" (1894-17 Sep 1927) married Bertha
   "Bert" Sanderson, 16 Jun 1915. Sandy was murdered. James
   Ellsworth Chavis discovered his body lying on the railroad
   tracks. He had been beaten with a blunt object [an axe] and
   his eyes had been removed.

Sandy, Jr., and Bertha's Children:

1j1. James Robert (14 Oct 1918-6 Dec 1993) married Strawdie
   Locklear; Butler (23 Dec 1916-26 May 1988) married Eula
   Mae Locklear; Archie (20 Oct 1926-20 Dec 1953) married
   Martha Jane Ransom; Franklin (16 Feb 1925-?) married Em-
   mert Barton. Franklin's second wife, Mazzell Brewer (9 Apr
   1924-26 Apr 2004); Mae (6 Oct 1926-?) married Stacy Hunt;
   and, Sanford (12 Aug 1922-2 Jan 1982), never married.

1k. John J. (12 Jan 1900-17 Dec 1960) married Cora Lee "Lela"
   Hammonds (14 Jun 1905-4 Feb 1999), 1927. Her parents were:
   Rev. S.A. Hammonds and Sarah Margaret Bell, a member to
   the Pvt. Samuel Bell's family.

John J. and Lela's Children:

1k1. Earl Cordell married Lorraine Burnette; John Mark "Mark" (23 Oct 1934-14 Mar 1981) married Betty Rose Oxendine; Maggie Lois (17 Sep 1930-9 Jul 2016) married Alvin Mercer; Vivian "Vib"; Stephen Andrew "Steve" (12 Aug 1941-20 Dec 1962); Superior Court Judge, Sandy Dexter (May 1945- 5 March 2002); and, Larry Trent (8 Oct 1946). Neither Steve nor Sandy Dexter ever married.

1l. Peter "Pete" (29 Apr 1902-1 Mar 1974) married Attie Mae Cummings, whose parents were: James "Jimmy" Cummings and Celester Maynor. Jimmy's parents were: Virginia Cummings and Henderson Oxendine. Jimmy's brother was John Nance Cummings.

Pete and Attie's Children:

1l1. Althaea (25 Nov 1924-8 Aug 2011) married Maynor; Nettie (22 Jan 1926-23 Mar 1984) married Seavie Lowry; Martin Luther (19 Apr 1929- 4 Jan 2018) married Carter; Martin remarried (NKA); Daphina (2 Jul 1927-29 Aug 2012) married Otis Locklear; Bernice married Marvin Lowery; Joyce Neil (26 Jun 1932) married Waltz Maynor; her second husband was Sampson; Dalton Peter (21 Apr 1936-13 Jan 2012); James Grady "Jimmy" (18 Jan 1934-26 Nov 2006); Ronald (30 Apr 1938) married Meskil Wilkins; Paul (12 Jun 1939) married Pauline Sampson; and, Howard Dearl (23 Jul 1941) married Brenda Brewington; his second wife, Brenda Lowry.
Marvin Lowery served in the US Army in WWII. He was a prisoner of war (POW).
Pete's second wife, Anna Belle Oxendine Sampson (20 Oct 1914-?), the daughter of James T. Oxendine and Mary Graham.

Pete and Anna Belle's Children:

112. Ernest Ray, Veril (d. 2019), and David who is recognized as the first American Indian veterinarian in Robeson County.

1m. Joseph "Joe" (6 Jan 1905-15 Feb 1980) married Sally Johnson (6 Oct 1905-24 Oct 1996).

Joe and Sally's Children:
1ml. Lucy Cynthia (19 Jan 1929) married Keys; Joan Patricia (5 Jun 1933) married Archie Cleave Baker; Stephen Anthony "Tony," (30 Aug 1939); and, Sherman married Deborah Deese, whose grandparents were: Conley Ransom and Cottie Lowrie. Joe's second wife was Mable (NKA).

Mittie's Children- Fathers unknown:

A. Susan "Little Susie" Brooks (1853-31 Aug 1937) was killed accidently by a train as she was attempting to cross the railroad tracks [present day Fuller's restaurant] to return home from tossing out a dead chicken into the woods near her home in Pembroke.

Susan married Archibald W. Locklear, the son of Knowel "Noel" Locklear, the son of Lovedy Johnson. Noel married Polly Lowrie. In the 1910 census, Susan was listed as a divorcee; she had given birth to (11) children but only three children survived. In 1930 census, she was listed as a widow.

1. Little Susie and Arch's Children:
    Maggie Lena, Ruthie, and Hamiah Lowry.
    1a. Maggie Lena Brooks Locklear (10 Apr 1898-10 Feb 1964), married Harley "Horkey" Oxendine.

    Maggie's Children:

    1a1. Marbell (11 Mar 1911-2 Mar 1963) and Martin Luther Smith's Children:
        1a1a. Carol married Alonzo Oxendine.

1a1b. Lancelot "Lance" Chavis (10 Dec 1927- 10 Nov 2003).
1a1c. Thelma married Bricey Hammonds, Jr.
1b. Ruthie (1898-23 Feb 1966) married Luther Waters Scoggins. In the 1930 census, she was listed as the wife of Charlie Berry.
1c. Hamiah Lowry (1877-3 May 1958). He died instantly from head injuries when struck by a pick-up truck while walking along NC Hwy 711. He never married.

B. [John] Wesley Locklear (1854-?) at a young age was murdered while harvesting turpentine. He never married. He was listed in both the 1870 and 1880 Robeson County census. He failed to appear in later censuses. Writer discovered a Wesley Locklair, born in SC abt. 1854. In the SC 1880 census, Wesley was (26) years-of-age. He was a Cooper, working in turpentine. Writer failed to discover additional information.

Mittie married Philip Jones Locklear (1848-20 Jun 1945), 16 Jan 1868. Philip was the son of Richmond "Richard" Locklier and Matilda Jones. Matilda was the daughter of Elias Jones. According to the Brooks family history, Mittie chose to returned to her maiden name, Mittie Brooks, when Philip married Martha Oxendine.

A. Mittie married Philip Jones Locklear.
1. Mittie and Philip's Children:
Alamenia (1867-1953); Narcissa "Nancy J." (1877-1965; Matilda (27 Oct 1880-12 Mar 1962); Adeline (1878-1962; Jesse (1864); and, Ebenezer "EB" (15 Jul 1871-20 Jul 1959).
Matilda married Lunnie Locklear (6 Dec 1873-14 Apr 1963), the son of Archibald and Elizabeth "Betsy" Lowrie.
EB married Nealia Cummings (1876), 22 Dec 1894, Robeson County, NC.
1a1. EB and Nealia's Children:
1a1a. Leacy Cummings Brooks (1896-26 Jan 1925) married Millard Locklear. EB married Avella Jacob (8 May 1890-Mar 1978), 6 Dec 1912, the daughter of Edith "Edy" Jacobs and Mitch Mitchell.
1a2. EB and Avella's Children: Gola (1902); Clara (1913);

Plummer (11 Aug 1916-10 Oct 1973) married Lois Locklear; twins: Lata May (14 Apr 1921-16 Apr 1921) and Nancy (born dead 14 Apr 1921); Viola (1918); Redell (d. 25 Jul 1972) married Shirley O. Oxendine; and, Matilda (1915-d.) married Cornelius Hocker [military].

1b.   Matilda and Lunnie Locklear's Children:
1b1.Dorothy Lee (19 Jan 1914-aliv.) married a Clark. On 19 Jan 2019, she is (106) years-of-age.
1b2.Debur [Deborah] Locklear (1904-1943) married Eddie Lee Revels (1906-18 Nov 1942).
1b2q.Willie Ree Revels.
1b3.Lonnie Lockler (1920).

Lunnie Locklear (6 Dec 1873-14 Apr 1963) parents were: Archibald and Betsy Lowrie Locklear. Archibald's second wife was Martha Locklear Cummings, the former wife of Troy Cummings, the son of Progenitor Enoch Cummins.

Philip Locklear Jones married Martha Oxendine.

A.   Philip and Martha's Children:
1.   Willoughby, William Luther Jones, and Lucy.
1a1.Willoughby married Mae Branch Shepherd.
1a2.William Luther Jones married Flora Branch.
1a3 Lucy Jones (1863) married a Sanderson. Their son was Lacy Sanderson. Lucy lived in the home of Richmond and Peggie Locklear.
1a3a.Vardell Sanderson married Hattie Locklear, the daughter of Eula Mae [Woriax] Locklear.
2.   Martha Oxendine's son:
2a.   Eddie Oxendine (16 Apr 1891-27 Jan 1973). He never married.

John Brooks participation in two battles:

The Battle of Camden, SC, 16 Aug 1780 and the Battle of Hobkirk Hill, 25 Apr 1781. It has been suggested that John Brooks may have served in the second battle but unlikely he served in the Battle of Camden, SC. It is documented that the Bladen County Militia took part in the battle at Charles Town, SC. Also, documentation reveals that John Brooks was released prior to the siege and surrender of the city of Charles Town, SC, 12 May 1780.

John Brooks Disposition applying for Military Pension:

John Brooks gave the following disposition as having served in the Militia and fought under Captain Alex McNull, Captain Gibson, Capt. Hadly at Camden, Betties Bridge, and made three tours to Charleston, SC. He was held as prisoner in Charleston, SC. Other witnesses to his disposition were - Jessy Jones, Tempsy Brooks, and Nancy Locklear (100 years-of-age). Rachel Brooks (abt. 90 years-of-age), swore she had known John Brooks for the last 85 years. Rachel Locklear (abt. 90 years-of-age), stated that she had known John Brooks for the last 80 years. Also, Rhody Locklear and Rachel Brooks.

Petition was filed with the Pension Office, Pension approved by William J. Clark, 8 September 1853.

John Brooks, a soldier in the Revolutionary War:

On 26 February, 1855 and additional dates, John Sinclair, JP, testified that he knew said John Brooks (between 95-100 years of age) and had known him for about 25 years. That John Brooks had fought in the war for about four years. In addition, Sinclair testified on 4 January 1854, that John Brooks had conveyed, that he [John Brooks], the Captain, and two others were taken as prisoners for about four months. Brooks stated they almost starved to death prior to the end of the war. The rest of his tour was spent around Wilmington, Cape Fear area. Sinclair's sworn testimony was reliable and witnessed by Thomas A. Norment and Shadrach Howell, JP, 1 March 1855, Robeson County, Lumberton, NC.

John Brooks Final Pension Articles:

Final Pension for John Brooks [S. 6732, 1858 North Carolina, M804, 353, 83], Agency: Fayetteville, NC, date of act 1832, date of payment 2d qr. 1861. Final Payment, GSA C 17-1935 GSA Dec 69 7068 and Final Payment Vouchers Index for Military Pensions, 1818-1864, Fold3.

Below is a letter written by *A.W. McLean*, president Bank of Lumberton, Lumberton, NC, Letter dated Sept 14, 1914, written to the Honorable Commissioner of Indian Affairs, Dept. of the Interior, Washington, DC

> Several of these Indians served in the Revolutionary War. John Brooks was granted a pension by the United States Government for services in the Revolutionary War. (See warrant No. 80030, issued to John Brooks for 160 acres of bounty land for his services in the Revolutionary War. See also Revolutionary War pension file No. 6732, pension order.) In Volume XXII of the North Carolina State Records, pages 56 and 57, it appears that the following Indians of Robeson County received a pension from the Government for service in the Revolutionary War: John Brooks, James Brooks, Berry Hunt, Thomas Jacobs, Michael Revells, Richard Bell, Samuel Bell, Primas Jacobs, Thomas Cummings, and John Hammond, these pensions having been granted under the Federal acts of 1818 and 1832.

George Washington Lowrie further states that he knew old John Brooks well, having seen him a number of times before he died. This John Brooks was a soldier in the Revolutionary War. (See application for pension in the records of the War Department at Washington.) Wash Lowrie says that old John Brooks died at the age of about 110 years. His application for pension states that he was about 90 or 96 years old when the pension was granted. Says that he was told by Aaron Revels, then 100 years old, and Daniel Lowrie, then 73 years old, and Joe Chavis, age 90 that these Indians in Robeson County came from Roanoke, in Virginia. That after remaining in Robeson County for some time they went to the mountains with the other Cherokees, but a number returned on account of leaving relatives in Robeson County, where they had mixed with other tribes and probably with several white families.

Indian Agent was O. M. McPherson

Final Pension for John Brooks, Agency: Fayetteville, NC, date of act 1832, date of payment 2d qr. 1861. Final Payment, GSA C 17-1935 GSA Dec 69 7068.[49]

The above Aaron Revels married Anna Rodgers, 27 Oct 1841.

---

[49] A.W. McLean.

SUMMARY AND CONCLUSION

This writer is limited in expressing honor and admiration for her Patriot War hero, John Brooks, Bladen County, NC. Secondly, she is thankful to her parents, Bontford "BF" Cummings and Lettie Mae Brooks, who insisted that she and her siblings knew who their ancestors were. Parents and relatives shared precious memories of former family members with her as a young child. Therefore, she was given a special knowledge of ancestors that many others failed to receive.

The valuable knowledge of John Brooks and William [Loughry] Lowrie and their dedication and loyalty to their country, America, seeking freedom from the rule of England, has always made a great impression in her life knowing that her ancestors who were yet considered citizens of America, were willing to, and fought bravely with others for freedom is truly an honor.

The life story of both Brooks and Loughry were powerful tools for writer in seeking and becoming a member of the National Society Daughters of the Revolution, Col. Thomas Robeson Chapter, Lumberton, NC.

On March 3, 2018, the Brooks family held a Celebration and Honor gathering to honor their ancestor Pvt. John Brooks at Prospect United Methodist Church, 3929 Missouri Rd. Maxton, NC. On September 4, 2018, Pvt. Samuel Bell direct descendants joined Pvt. John Brooks direct descendants, members of the Robeson County Sons of the Revolution (SAR), and the Col. Thomas Robeson Chapter in placing the John Brooks' Daughters of the American Revolution War (NSDAR) Grave Marker in the Bear Swamp Baptist Church Cemetery, Eureka Road, Pembroke, NC. The marker rests beside Lettie Mae Brooks Cummings' grave. Lettie Mae was (5x) great-granddaughter of John Brooks and the mother of Rev. Dr. Carolyn Cummings-Woriax, a member of the Colonel Thomas Robeson NSDAR Chapter, Lumberton, NC.

BIBLIOGRAPHY

Apess, William. *On Our Ground: The Complete Writings of William Apess, A Pequot.* Editors Colin G. Calloway, and Barry O'Connell. United States of America: University of Massachusetts Press, 1992.

Barnhill, Jane Blanks, *Sacred Grounds162 Lumbee Cemeteries in Robeson County,* 2007, p. 6. (*Lumbee Library*.appstate.edu/files/Britt-2pdf, 26 Dec 2015.)

Bennett, Ivan L., ed., *Song and Service Book for Ship and Field: Army and Navy.* Chairman of the Editorial Committee, United States Government Printing Office, Washington, 1942. Copyright, 1941, by A. S. Barnes and Company, Incorporated.

Bladen County Tax List, 1768 and 1774. NC Library of Archives and History, Raleigh, NC, 11 Aug 2015.

_____. 1763 Tax List Bladen County, GR929.3 N8be S497, p. 3. NC Library of Archives and History, Raleigh, NC, 11 Aug 2015.

Branson's North Carolina Business Directory, Robeson County facts and figures. (https://interactive.ancestry.com/10160dvm.)

Bumgarner, Reverend George William. *Methodist Episcopal Church in North Carolina 1865-1939.* Winston-Salem: Hunter Publishing Co., 1990.

Col. Lytle. The Sons of the American Revolution (NSSAR) le Marquis de Lafayette Chapter, Fayetteville, NC.

Cummings-Woriax, Carolyn. *Bladen & Robeson Counties: Early Land Deeds.* Non-published.

_____. *Teaching A Study in The Wesleyan Tradition on Holiness of Heart & Life.* Doctor of Ministry Project. Hood Theological Seminary, Salisbury, NC, May 2013.

_____. *The Creation of An Innovative People 1700-1887: The Shaping of a New Territory: Robeson County, NC.* Non-published.

_____. *The Early American Indian Patriots and Soldiers Roster in North Carolina and South Carolina.* Non-published.

_____. *The Historical Bell Family.* Non-published.

_____. *The John "Johnie" Brooks Family.* Non-published.

_____. Final Pension for John Brooks, Agency: Fayetteville, NC, date of act 1832, date of payment 2d qr. 1861. Final Payment, GSA C 17-1935 GSA Dec 69 7068].

Gammon, David B. *Records of Estates, Warren County, NC,* Vol. 1, 1780-1805. Raleigh, NC, 1988.

Gregg, DD., The Right Rev. Alexander. *History of the Old Cheraws: Containing An Account of the Aborigines of the Pedee The First White Settlements Their Subsequent Progress, Civil Changes, the Struggle of the Revolution, and Growth of the Country Afterward Extending from About A.D. 1730-1810.* Columbia, S.C: The State Company, 1905.

Grundset, Eric G. Ed. and Project Manager. *Forgotten Patriots: African American & Native American Patriots Appendix of the North Carolina Daughters of American Revolutionary War Soldier.* North Carolina, n.d.

Hawks, Francis L. *History of North Carolina: with maps and illustrations*, Vol. 1 & Vol. II, Fayetteville, N.C.: E.J. Hale & Son, 1858.

Heinegg, Paul. *Free African Americans of Virginia, North Carolina, South Carolina, Maryland, and Delaware*. Named in the Robeson County Court Minutes 1797-1843.

Hicks, Theresa M., Ed. *South Carolina Indians Indian Traders and Other Ethnic Connections beginning in 1670*. Spartanburg, South Carolina: Published for Peppercorn Publications, Inc by The Reprint Company, Publishers, 1998.

Locklear, Grady. *Genealogy: A Perspective: Carter, Chavis, Cummings, Hunt, Locklear, Lowery, and Sampson Family Tree*. n.d.

Freedom of the City Admission Papers 1681-1930. London, England, (database on line), 2010. (https://www.ancestry.com operations, Inc. accessed: 14 Oct 2019.)

Loyalists in the Southern Campaign of the Revolutionary War, Vol. 1, p. 153, Captain Peter Tyler's, SC Loyal Militia, 1 September 1780-1 September 1782, 730 days, Camden, SC. (https://www.ancestry.com accessed: 5 Oct 2015.)

McLean, A.W., president Bank of Lumberton, Lumberton, NC, Letter dated September 14, 1914, written to the Honorable Commissioner of Indian Affairs, Dept of the Interior: Washington, DC.

_____. *Semi-Weekly Robesonian Newspaper* article, "Historical Sketch of Indians of Robeson County," April 1913, p. 7.

Militia, Vouchers for Soldiers in the Continental Line, 1783-1792.

Mills, Elizabeth Shown. *Evidence Explained: Citing History Sources from Artifacts to Cyberspace*, 2nd ed., Revised 2012.

Military Records. (https://www.fold3.ancestry.com accessed: 30 Sep 2019.)

National Archives and Records Administration, Record Group 75, Entry 616, Box 14/15—North Carolina, Raleigh, NC, March 3, 2018.

Norment, Mary C. *The Lowie History*. Lumberton: Lumbee Printing Company, 1909.

North Carolina Daughters of American Revolution War (NSDAR) Register.

North Carolina Marriage Records, 1741-2011. (https://www.ancestry.com accessed: 24 Jul 2019.)

North Carolina State Library, Raleigh, NC, August 2 & 11, 2015.

Robeson County Courthouse Land Deeds Office, Land Deed 6 T, p.175, Aaron Brooks Last Will and Testament.

Robeson County 1850 Southern Division census, dwelling #100, family #100, Alfred Townsend. Mary Cumboe, age 75, pauper. (https://www.ancestry.com accessed: 31 Jul 2017, 12:30 AM.)

Robeson County Court Minutes 1797-1843 List: "Hardy Bell listed as a Boy of Color bound to Samuel Bell," 27 Aug 1810.

Robeson County Mortality Schedule, 1880. (https://www.ancestry.com.)

Roster of Soldiers from North Carolina in the American Revolutionary, 1700, pp. 314-318. (https://www.ancestry.com accessed: 31 Jul 2017, 12:30 am.)

Roster of Soldiers from North Carolina in the American Revolution. Clark's State Records, p. 527, col. 13. (https://www.ancestry.com accessed: 31 Jul 2017, 12:30 am.)

Roster of North Carolina Soldiers serving in the Revolutionary War. North Carolina State Library Archives, Raleigh, NC and New Hanover Library Archives, Wilmington, NC.

Sampson County Courthouse Land Deeds Office, Deed Book, p. 886, 6 Feb 1804, Mary Bell's Last Will and Testament.

Smith, Lula Jane, and Joseph Michael Smith, eds. *The Lumbee Methodist: Getting to Know Them*. Raleigh: The Commission of Archives and History NC Methodist Conference, 1990.

South Carolina History and Archives Library. Columbia, SC.

Southern Campaign American Revolution Pension Statement & Rosters – John Brooks S6732.

State-Wide, NC – Revolutionary War Pensioners, 1859. *The Raleigh Standard*, Aug 24, 1859. North Carolina Roll of Honor – John Brooks, Robeson County, 102 years.

The 1767 Cumberland County Census Substitutes Index 1790-1890. (https://www.ancestry.com.)

The Gilbert Family Cemetery, Toomsboro, GA. (https://www.ancestry.com.accessed.)

The North Carolina Central and Fayetteville Gazette Newspaper, 1795. Nancy Oxendine. (https://www.ancestry.com accessed: 20 Jul 2017.)

The NC Daughters of American Revolutionary War Soldiers, Appendix, *North Carolina African Americans and American Indians in the Revolutionary Era*, "Forgotten Patriots."

The Robeson County Area. *The Historical News*. Hiram, GA., April 2019, p. 7.

The *Revolutionary War Soldier's Pension Books*. New Hanover Library, Wilmington, NC and North Carolina State Library, Raleigh, NC.

The Second North Carolina Regiment Company B and the 2nd North Carolina Militia.

The U.S. School Catalogs, 1765-1935 for Hardy Holmes, p. 64 (1820), NC Un of NC, 1795. (https://www.ancestry.com.)

Turabin, Kate L. A Manual for Writers of Term Papers, Theses, and Dissertations, 7th ed. Chicago: University of Chicago Press, 2007.

Webb, Mable Jacobs Locklear. *The Robert Locklear Family Genealogy Book*. March 11, 2006. Self-published.

_____. *The Nathan Jacobs Family Book*. March 11, 2006. Self-published.

Williams, Ruth Smith, and Margarette Glenn Griffin. *Abstracts of Wills, Edgecombe, NC 1733-1856*. Old Edgecombe County Historical Library: Asheville, NC, 30 Oct 2017.

US Federal Census 1820, Cumberland County, NC. (https://www.ancestry.com.)

US Federal Census 1860, Cumberland County, NC. (https://www.ancestry.com.)

US Federal Census 1860, Robeson County. (https://www.ancestry.com accessed: 20 Aug 2016.)

US Federal Census 1880, Lafayette, Indiana. (https://www.ancestry.com.)

U.S. Federal Census Mortality Schedule, 1850-1885, Robeson County, NC. (https://www.ancestry.com.)

U.S. Federal Census Mortality Schedule, 1850-1885, Sampson County, NC. (https://www.ancestry.com.)